KEYS to UNCOMFORTABLE LIVING

GARRELL—

ORIGINALITY IS JUST
A TIRED IDEA IN FRONT
OF THE RIGHT PEOPLE.

THANKS FOR YOUR SUPPORT.

Bob Woo

KEYS *to* UNCOMFORTABLE LIVING

AN INDULGENCE OF MY PECULIARITIES, AN INDICTMENT OF YOURS

BY

BOB WOODIWISS

emmis
books

!

Thousands of Things Had to Go Wrong for Me to Get Here
Acknowledgments

Have there been mistakes? Absolutely. Miscues? Certainly. False starts, errors in judgment, misunderstandings, failures, tail-chasing, inadequacies, ineptitudes, sloth, cowardice? Yes, all those. Many times over. And that's just my day so far—the nasty, treacherous, deeply potholed washboard of a road that stretches from the beginning of this paragraph to precisely-y-y-y-y-y-y-y-y-y...here! To say "I fail myself more before 9 A.M. than most people do all day" comes far closer to being the absolute truth than it does to being brazen copyright infringement.

But to me, that's the writing process. Torturous. Frustrating and defeating. A constant struggle between choosing the wrong word and choosing the wronger word. One sentence written, two sentences deleted, as it were. Honestly, if writing were any more of a daily torment to me, I'd say it must be a Republican president.

So it's not hard to believe then that, even though I decided I wanted to be a writer at age fourteen, it took over three decades to finally finish a book and get it published. (Yeah, *this* book, Special Eds and Edwinas.) Now, the only items I have left on my To Do Before Death List are "Legitimize my secret identity by acquiring some superpower(s)," (also put on the list at age fourteen) and "Cheer up!" (something I've wanted to do since I was twenty-six).

But let's not lose sight of the fact that a book *has* happened.

And while its creation, writing, and publication may to a large extent exist *despite* my particularly thick brain soup of meta-self-consciousness, low self-esteem, inordinate doubt, fearfulness, generalized anxiety, neuroses, indolence, plus a secret blend of thirteen other as yet unidentified though fully functional and piquant psychological and emotional flaws and spices, it also exists *because* of it, i.e., it is only *because* of this fiasco of a psyche that I have anything to say at all. And it is only via the afore-alluded to missteps, nonsteps, and long strides of retreat dictated by my grab bag of personal deficiencies that I now reach, however circuitously or belatedly or unlikely, this authorial summit. (Am I the only one who's bored here? How about we all close our eyes for a few minutes and imagine a car chase through the cement canyon and shallow waters of the Los Angeles River... SCREEEEEE! SPLASHCRASH! BAH-BOOM! OK. I'm rejuiced. Back to business.)

Of course, no book is written by a single author. By which I mean, I have no intention of hogging all the credit for creating my disastrous self or, by extension, this, its lexical spawn. So, for their invaluable help and contributions, I would like to thank the following:

The Partner. What can I say? I realize my progress was unbearably slow, my passion for the work frequently dubious, my lack of ambition persistently vexing and my hit-and-miss employment financially crippling. But then, as my mate, you've been an accessory to my every failure and failing. The fact that, throughout our marriage, you regularly pressured me into seeking psychological counseling helped keep me in touch with the fact that I'm a miserable, bent, and contemptible fuck who, to stay within the parameters of your love limits, had better dump a lot of his bullshit in the lap of paid strangers.

Dad, from the time I first became interested in writing, you explicitly expressed your complete lack of faith in my ability and prospects. Without that doubt and disapproval, I likely would have missed the colorful, shameless, and shameful years of drug and alcohol abuse that were so instrumental in (eventually) shaping my voice and work. Worse, had I had your moral and emotional support, I would in all likelihood have foolishly dedicated myself to pursuing my dream and, perhaps, become an author sooner rather than later. "Foolishly" because I realize now that any success which might have come my way early on, when I was a young man, would have been wasted, that my immaturity would have precluded me from fully appreciating the achievement, the recognition, the rewards, awards, and accolades. No, Dad, without the thirty-year run-up to the publication of this book, I would certainly have been deprived of my current feeling of undying gratitude for the low-ball advance and tepid attentions some desperate, pitying publisher has thrown my way.

Mom, don't for a minute think you weren't a huge help, too. You were. Throughout my boyhood, your forthright devotion to preparing and assembling overabundant meals of red meat, starches, fats, oils, and sugar along with your cooings of "Have another helping" and "Come on and finish this up" and "There's plenty more," produced a much larger, more padded and comfortable ass for me to sit on and write. Even more importantly, for the past few years, the years I've been working on this book, your total disinterest in what I've been doing or how it was going gave me the freedom to guiltlessly ignore you and your so-called needs so I could get on with not just my work but my life.

Had it not been for my two sisters, with their alternating deep-seated resentment of and emotional detachment from me, I might have known the joys of sibling affection and the bonds of shared experience and wound up writing the kind of drippy, sappy, treacly family crap I absolutely refuse to even read. Thanks, girls, for not letting *that* train wreck happen.

To my feckless acquaintances and colleagues, I truly appreciate that by never actually becoming my friends you reinforced my bleak worldview, saving me the time and energy it would have taken to reassess and reevaluate. Also, your infrequent and hollow words of encouragement made me want to finish this book all the more, so I could rub your disbelieving faces in it.

For those who saw fit to publish my work in the past, your preposterously low pay kept my writing free of the taint of commercialism while your nonexistent readership ensured I could not pander to an audience; and for all my editors over the years, I give a gratefull nod of acknowledgment for there scrupulous atttention too detial.

There are also several exceptional educators who made a contribution to this book. Mr. Chesowitz, my gym teacher from fourth through eighth grade, who, through his example, inspired me to enter some field where I could wear shorts to work. Mr. Bostrich, who, through his lack of a discernable personality and nonexistent communication skills, failed to fill my head with New Math so I could fill it with something useful. Ms. Kleeman, my ninth-grade English teacher and the woman who paralyzed me for years by planting in my head the idea that there is no sentence a preposition can come at the end of. Ms. Mazurki, whose lack of control over her History class allowed me, the class clown, to run roughshod over the other students and prove to myself that making people cry at the hands of humor is easy, enjoyable, and largely unpunishable. And finally,

Dr. Fonsk, my History of Western Civilization professor and the author of the text he required students to use in his class, the man who proved to me that lucidity and education are inversely proportional and that I better stop while I was ahead.

The time I spent at the writers' support group, Critique, which I attended exactly twice, was invaluable. To hear you, my fellow aspiring writers, offer such generous critiques of, enthusiasm for, and positive feedback on each other's stories and chapters told me that if *writers* were so undiscerning, so easily snookered, *readers* would be a piece of cake. But what was truly inspiring was to read your work and come to the realization that while my work might end up on some publishing slush pile, it wouldn't be at the *bottom* of the slush pile.

To my many employers over the years, by treating me with disrespect, discourtesy, and condescension, you forced me to remain sharply focused on my one true goal: Do something, *anything,* in order to escape the rule of tin pot despots who liberally dispense fear and dull routine in the service of soulless companies. And whether you were my overlord in a numbingly tawdry retail store or a dark, dank warehouse, a drunkard-lined bar or a drunkard-lined ad agency, your carefree unfairness and crazy quilt of adamant contradictions demonstrated to me that making sense isn't a prerequisite for making money.

I am indebted to the City of Cincinnati. Its unwavering conservatism combined with its relentless cynicism taught me that it's bad to color outside the lines but good to criticize the picture. Its parochialism always made me feel like an outsider but its tradition of overzealous prosecutors and fascistic law enforcement made me think twice before allowing this feeling of alienation to manifest itself as violent or destructive behavior and instead channel it into harmless, malicious mockery. Its lack of forward progress gave me the illusion I was moving.

Lorne Michaels, for decades I looked at the TV programs and films you produced and asked, "Will this man never make me laugh?" Thank you for creating and succeeding with a new kind of comedy: the kind no one laughs at. For a guy like me, that lowers the bar to a level I can approach with, if not confidence, condescension.

Lastly, I acknowledge my great debt to God. The world You've created is to me as a grain of sand is to an oyster: highly irritating, but it's what I have to work with.

PART III.
ON THE OUTSIDE LOOKING INSOLENT

My World and Wipe Your Feet When You Come In.
An Introduction

I live an uncomfortable life. Not unhappy or dissatisfied or seething. Uncomfortable. Entirely survivable, scarcely convivial. Like, say, driving cross-country with Nancy Reagan. Put less succinctly, I see my daily slog as a labyrinthine quagmire of a shipwreck with doubt, awkwardness, and irritation lurking down every dead end of a dark alley.

I attribute this overall dissettlement to six basic sources: people, events, institutions, issues, processes, and, of course, et cetera. Within those few broad categories, however, lie a swarm of specifics: from the abridgement of civil liberties in the face of terrorism to the dreary inescapability of at least one visit to RadioShack every year. From unproven FrankenFoods with their modified DNA to the disturbing menagerie who shares my DNA. From the depersonalizing effects of technology to the hyperpersonalizing effects of Toastmasters International. From buying a car to renting a wig. From the linguistic metahelixes of investment prospecti to keeping up with the ceaseless ebb and flow of fashionable necktie width. From the politics of the ruling party (whomever it may be) to Cher's disastrously brief marriage to Gregg Allman. (This list, due to space constraints, must remain a mere bird dropping on the tip of the proverbial iceberg.)

Worse, I'm increasingly bothered by the fact that such stuff has the power to bother me, plus I'm bothered by the too silent/too strident people who, like me, are also bothered, but, I hasten to add, even more so by the ones who are not.

In other words, my doctor says Mylanta. A remedy to be slugged down, he suggests, in conjunction with electroshock therapy.

But enough about me. Let's negatively assess you.

You're uncomfortable, too. You have to be. Because the same people who watch reality TV shows, go to action film trilogies, and read *Left Behind* books are allowed to vote. Because you know it's only a question of time before white guys are sporting Afros again. Because there's no way to politely decline a proffered high five. Because opportunity still knocks but, for a variety of reasons, no longer ventures outside America's gated communities. Because hanging a No Pest Strip on the front porch doesn't keep away the Jehovah's Witnesses. Because if tomorrow is a brighter day, we're undoubtedly hurtling toward the sun. Because while there's no such thing as a dumb question, dumb questioners are everywhere you fucking go. Because baby talk doesn't count as a second language. Because yesterday's slaughterhouse is today's herd downsizing facility. Because pompous writers feel free to blindly spout their doubts about a reader's ability to adequately cope with society, culture, and structure. Because this is America. Because this is Earth. Because time moves at a constant speed and in a single direction.

Of course, we're not all created equally uneasy. Each of us has our own personal discomfort level, our own tolerances and triggers. (For instance, your idea of Hell might be a Loggins & Messina reunion while mine might be one by Seals & Crofts. Or maybe I think horsewhipping is too good for Tom DeLay and you think it's a good place to start.) But regardless of how much or how little uncertainty, inadequacy, perplexity, and perturbity you and I may suffer on a daily basis, the fact is, with this book, I finally found a way to make money on mine.

And with that, I'm completely comfortable.

1} Hostile-ry

Check-in chafes. I can't simply be polite, I have to be friend-ly. I can't merely transact business, I have to meet our "hosts." I can't just be interested in getting to our room, I have to feign interest in the house and grounds, and grasp "how breakfast works." Thus, I'm reminded that vacationing at a bed-and-breakfast is always much harder work than the work it's supposed to provide a vacation from.

We're here because The Partner loves B & Bs. She also claims to love me. That these two paradoxical loves can exist in a single human vessel proves the existence of God. Or of multiple personality disorder.

Our room is overdecorated. Of course. Dark, ornate antiques compete so heavily for space I expect them to start throwing elbows. Frilly lampshades and curtains make a brazen but largely futile attempt to distract one's eye from the clashing, vertigo-inducing floral prints of comforter, upholstery, and wallpaper. Gracing various horizontal and vertical surfaces around the room are handmade craft items of faux stained glass, needlepoint, decoupage, appliqué, even tiny shells glued into the shapes of little people, each a reminder that the bric-a-brac arts are best left to the inmates of Chinese torture camps. (Theory: *The Antiques Roadshow,* riding the swell of a bipolar mood swing, seduced an absinthe-swilling issue of *Martha Stewart Living* and this room is their twisted mutant lovechild.)

Despite the fully overfull fulsomeness of the decor, however, the single most fundamental furnishing is missing. That is, the room has no TV. This, I know from bitter experience, is not the result of some cataclysmic blunder but rather of heartless intent. A forced return to the Victorian era. A return I'd mind a lot less in this instance if some laudanum came with it.

And the bathroom? The bathroom is all spun saccharine, with its dish of untouchable baby soaps, untouchable embroidered hand towels, and an un-tushable decorative crocheted commode cover. On the wall, a sampler featuring an outhouse genteelly alludes to an amusing aspect of urination. So, I think, standing there, taking it all in, Hell, it would seem, is ceramically tiled.

Making an exit here is troublesome. Troublesome because I can't seem to reach the sole door to the outside world without being buttonholed by our chronic, lurking host. "Where are you off to today?" "Has our kitty-cat wandered back to your room to check you out yet?" "Looks like you're going running. Reminds me of my son, he used to be on the track team. Then, after he graduated, the little fool fell in with the wrong crowd and robbed a gas station. Blames me, of course, his upbringing, like kids will. Swears now that he's outta jail he's gonna come back here and burn this place down with me in it . . ." "Does this look infected to you?" The Partner tells me these free-flowing discursions are spontaneous, harmless, diverting; I tell her they're assault with a deadly personality.

I sleep fitfully in the too-short, antique four-poster bed. (I'm confused: If the simian-to-human evolutionary transition was more or less completed tens of thousands of years ago, why is it that, all the way up through the nineteenth century, the length of the average bed was only sufficient to comfortably accommodate a supine chimpanzee?) Its tired wooden frame and slats protest with a long, low groan when I roll over on the lumpy mattress. In the morning I discover that the noise and lumps weren't the bed at all. I'd rolled over and smothered the aforementioned inquisitive kitty-cat.

And what would our B & B stay be without breakfast? (I suppose, it would be a stay at a B, or, perhaps, at a B & No-B, or, possibly, the negative B of the non-Breakfast would cancel out the positive B of the Bed and we'd simply be staying at a "O," but I digress.) This is a nasty affair. First, we're compelled to share a table with four other guests—total strangers! All looking crisp, well-rested and Republican! And wearing madras!—a practice I'd assumed had (sensibly) died in the roadhouses of the Middle Ages. Second, we are served and attended by our hosts who hover and jabber and urge to such an excruciating extent that I find myself longing wistfully to be a black man eating at Denny's. Third, I don't want dried fruit compote and Eggs Bangladesh and millet/pumpkin seed/cranberry granola and yam hash browns and mango slurry and cinnamon-raisin decaf at this hour of the morning. All I want is a triple espresso. Preferably pushed in front of me from the kitchen by a mute with a long stick.

Fourth, did I mention that people wear madras here?

Time to leave. Check out. Settle up the bill. I send The Partner to take care of this. I don't want to know how much this little adventure is setting us back. (Financially, I mean. I've already reckoned how much it's set back our relationship.) Next vacation, I tell myself, I'll insist we stay someplace with a twenty-first-century decor and a swift, humble, deferential staff. Which, I suppose, rules out France.

2} Flagging Interest

Dear Neighbor,

It has not escaped my attention that you, along with everyone else on the street, are flying the American flag far more often than in years past. I suspect that my failure to do the same may also have attracted yours. Please allow me to explain why my display of patriotism is so lacking:

1. I burned all my flags protesting something. Or things, I should say, though I don't remember what exactly. Probably I flambéed a few over nuclear proliferation; I was big on that for a while and I could get really get into a froth on the subject. And I torched plenty of them at free speech demonstrations; those rallies always got my flag-burning juices flowing. NAFTA and the WTO claimed a few, too. Honestly, though, a lot of my flags got ashed for less than noble reasons. I mean, burning them kind of became my "thing," my "signature." I lit 'em at my nephew's Little League games, at my high school

reunion, even one time at the grand opening of a Supercuts. Whatever, that big box of American flags I had in my basement is empty now.

2. I don't really need a flag in my yard since I recently stuck a teeny-tiny "window cling" decal of an American flag in the middle of my left contact lens. That way, I see a vague, translucent image of the Stars and Bars out in front of me all day long. Also, if I poke myself hard in the eye with my finger, the red and blue and purple spots I see look like fireworks going off behind Old Glory on the Fourth of July.

3. I'm just playing the angles. See, there's an Iraqi woman who works in my office and who I'm thinking about asking on a date. Her name's Shelly and she's an American citizen, not naturalized, either, second generation, and from what I've overheard in the break room, she deplores terrorism and weapons of mass destruction and the killing of our troops over there and <u>totally</u> supports this country's efforts to stop the first and third

things and find the second, but, geez,
she's really, really cute and I don't
want to do anything that could even
<u>remotely</u> associate me with this coun-
try's imperialistic hegemony of her
ancestral homeland and/or living
relatives and thereby hurt my chances
with or offend her if I ever get the
nerve to actually go out with her and,
you know, bring her back to my place
for coffee or a drink.

4. Stripes make my house look fat. I
keep hoping the government will come
out with a flag in a solid, muted earth
tone or, if they absolutely have to
have a print, a subtle houndstooth—you
know, something that'll look good on
your average Midwestern house, not just
on some skinny, New York brownstone.

5. My flagpole, made of black walnut,
manufactured in the 1920s, and rated
for forty-eight stars, is currently in
the shop being restored, updated, and
modified to accommodate the modern
fifty-star standard.

6. It's been almost three years since
you all started calling me "the lazy
ass who won't paint his house" and

I'm sick and tired of it. May I suggest you now switch to "the son of a bitch without the flag?"

7. As someone of Swiss descent, I find myself confronting this country's recurrent crises with nothing more than a swelling sense of neutrality.

8. You always expect me to play along with your little yard themes and schemes but you never go along with mine. Like, remember a few years ago? Somebody got a cement goose and dressed it up in different outfits and before you know it everybody's got a goose with outfits. It was practically mandatory. Then came the silhouettes. Of the dog barking up the tree, of the man leaning against the tree, etc., etc. And before this whole Old Glory kick, every house around here was all caught up in hanging holiday flags and special occasion flags and seasonal flags. And, hey, let's not forget the ironic flamingoes and gnomes. But how about when I replaced my garage door with strings of glass beads? Or when I turned the front yard into a prairie dog village? Or put the condom machine next to my mailbox? Where were you

"trend sheep" for those ideas? Nowhere, that's where. Well, I'm telling you, you provincial bastards, until somebody gets behind one of my ideas, screw you.

9. There are strict rules governing the hows and whens and wheres of displaying the United States flag, and if I were any good whatsoever at following strict rules, I wouldn't have a pair of cuticle scissors and three bottle caps lodged in my large intestine.

10. My habitual abuse of peyote renders me incapable of undertaking any job that would require my attention for any time period longer than ten angstroms in the cruel helix of wolf geography. Repiffens?

Yours sinceremoniously,

Bobobobobobobob

3} There Is No Right Man for the Job: An Unhandy Life in Three Phases

⊏▭■— Breaking Ground: A Shallow Pool of Talent

Neither Dad nor I was particularly handy, clever, or capable. We'd proved that the year we'd resodded the front yard green-side down. So the day he said I should grab the toolbox (contents: a ball peen hammer, two Phillips-head screwdrivers with palm-shredding grips, a nearly unliftable beast of a cast-iron monkey wrench inherited from my grandfather, a dinner knife, and an automobile jack) and meet him in the backyard, I foresaw nothing but shame and puncture wounds.

Out in the backyard, Dad stood next to a casket-sized carton. On it, the words *FinFest Pools* in watery-wavy letters were printed across a bright color photo of three sun-pinkened children tossing a beach ball in an above-ground swimming pool. That the kids were happy and unwounded told me they'd been off watching TV or driving go-carts while their deft, tool-rich father had swiftly, single-handedly erected their FinFest. To comfort myself, I decided their sanguine coloration was the result of a searing chlorine burn.

From the box we pulled bundles of tubular steel arcs, a tightly rolled band of blue corrugated steel, a thick mass of vinyl, struts, uprights, supports, clips, connectors, hangers, filters, thingees, whatzits, whozits, jarvels, klugs, mnoplochs, and framistans. Honestly, by the time the pieces were all unpacked, we looked like NTSB inspectors standing amidst the recovered wreckage of a jetliner crash.

"Whaddaya think?" Dad asked rhetorically. It had to be rhetorical because, since there was no way our collective twenty thumbs could possibly stuff Pandora's parts back into the box, we now had no choice but to begin trying to turn them into a swimming pool.

The instructions for assembly were, of course, of no use whatsoever. They required so much rereading, were so confounding, I'm convinced they were a lost work of James Joyce. Consequently, in an inspired moment of resignation, we threw them aside, deciding we might just as well tackle the pool itself. Or, as it would come to be known, The Cauldron of Malice.

Apparently, our FinFest was the product of a brilliant yet sinister mind—Lex Luthor, perhaps, or Antonin Scalia. Its intricacies, its subtleties, its cruel logic broke us as systematically as God broke Job, turning father against son and son against, well, by fifteen I was already against everything but it didn't do anything to help that.

As if our task wasn't oppressive enough, the warm morning sun had by now reached its zenith in the cloudless, late-summer sky. (Dad, who clung to his money more tightly than Madeline Murray O'Hare at a tent revival, had purchased the pool not in May but in the last days of August at an "End of Any Sane Person's Interest Sale.") The temperature topped ninety degrees. The humidity neared 100 percent. My only consolation was that this stifling combination had us steaming like high-class lobsters rather than grilling like the butt-end pork chops we were.

The way each of us chose to dress in this ugly heat was a study in contrast. I wore only shorts and high-top gym shoes, so that, as I shifted and lifted, the bulk and bulges of my shirtless torso flopped and quivered and cried to the world, "The child obesity epidemic is coming, the child obesity epidemic is coming." (Not until later did I learn the stinking, stinging, disgusting barrels of sweat that poured off me seriously contaminated the local aquifer.)

Dad, on the other hand, was, by anyone's estimation, over-dressed. His shoes were an ancient pair of wingtips, long retired from his office wardrobe, the leather uppers dry and stiff as a Paul Harvey punch line. Instead of shorts, he sported a pair of long, medium-weight, dark tan cotton slacks; the fact that my Dad only wore long pants was well established, and, as such, well beyond my interest to ask why. His shirt was a white T, gauze-thin and tucked into his pants. This item, I'd noticed, the old man reserved exclusively for "yard work," I suppose because it offered the lightness and freedom of movement required for his more typical outdoor jobs, like unfolding a chaise lounge and coiling the garden hose.

Dad's crowning sartorial accessory, as much a part of his "look" as black nylon stretch socks, was the smoldering, filterless Lucky Strike dangling from his lips. (That he was an incorrigible chain smoker was clear from the scar Mom bore on her cheek—evidently, years earlier, Dad had forgotten to remove it from his mouth when the minister said, "You may kiss the bride.") When he yawned, I could see that even his molars' silver fillings were tinted nicotine gold.

All things considered—the heat, the exertion, his get-up, the cigarettes—I fully expected Dad to keel over with a heart attack at any minute. But, forever a contrary man, he'd make me wait another eight years for that.

Frustrations mounted. Tempers erupted. As they did, we each became more determined. Willful. This job *would* get done. Because without the pool, there would be no place to drown each other.

We worked on. For hours. The sides collapsed more often than Judy Garland. The vinyl liner proved to be less far plastic than Liza Minnelli. And the filtration system was tougher to get up and running than Lorna Luft's career. Then, somehow, someway, with the sun about to wrap up its shadow-casting day, *mirabile dictu*, there, stable and standing was a three-and-a-half-foot-deep swimming pool. Yeah! Woodiwiss Men: 1, EMTs: 0!

It would take several hours for the pool to fill. Giving Dad and I time to cool off, collect ourselves, reflect on a job well done. Which we did until Mom came out and told us to "get the damn thing out of that tree."

Rough Framing: Useless from the White Collar Down

My back is neither broad nor strong. I have not worn a hard hat since Skylab stopped falling out of the sky. My hands are uncallused. I am not all thumbs, I am all thumb stumps. The major brand names in my toolbox are Oneida, Lady Craftsman, and Advil. If it ain't broke, I ain't fixed it. My handiness is so infinitesimal that it could not be picked up with needle-nose pliers—whatever the hell *they* are. A documentary of me using any given power tool could be marketed as an undiscovered "Fourth Stooge" movie. The clearest indication that I'm completely ill-suited to work in any of the building trades is that people like me don't make me sick.

I do not know the true dimensions of a two-by-four. I cannot tell a load-bearing wall from a carefree one. When in a situation where I have to decide between using screws or nails, I ask myself, "How the bloody hell did I get into this situation again?" Rather than "Measure twice, cut once," I "Measure thrice, call my therapist about fear of commitment." Statistically speaking, there's actually less likelihood I'll ever "put something in square" than there is I'll "put something in Tyra Banks." The popularity of body piercing has proved invaluable in masking my ineptitude with a nail gun. I'm pretty sure "sanding the upright" will make one go blind. I have a powerful desire to join two pieces of the same kind of wood but, according to *The Carpenter's Bible*, that would be an abomination. The hell with the furniture, my hands are full maintaining my personality's flimsy veneer.

Unsupervised, I will almost surely over-Drano. Though I may look in charge, the plumber's helper is the brains of the outfit. I strongly believe that there would be far fewer plumbing problems if water weren't so damn runny. In any analogy drawn between my home's plumbing system and the human urogenital system, I would be assigned the part of an enlarged, cancerous prostate gland. Pipe dope sure isn't what I thought it was. Ditto, fluxing a joint. The endless dripdripdripdripdrip of a leaky faucet has not driven me to the far side of madness since the night I frantically hacked off my ears. No, I don't understand why water drains counterclockwise in Australia, but an even bigger mystery to me is why their plumbers' asscracks are in the front. My general recklessness with a monkey wrench has made me the target of a defamation of character suit brought by four species of monkeys.

I cannot tell the hot wire from the ground wire from the wire I have no adjective for. Plugs are from Mars, outlets are from Venus. Is it merely a coincidence that extension cords with three-prong connections look like they're giving me the finger? It only takes one Bob to put in a light bulb. (Will that Bob please contact me in care of my publisher?) An overhead electrical fixture is over my head long before coming out of its box. I try never to stick a knife into a plugged-in toaster, even when I'm in the mood for a toasted knife. As a matter of personal compassion, I'm seriously considering having my wiring updated so that, just in case I make a serious error, instead of being fatally electrocuted, I'll be lethally injected.

There is poetry in the fact that a full 50 percent of the word "painting" is "pain." I see the paint as the yin, the roller as the yang, and me as the yutz. I am absolutely baffled as to where to put the drop cloth when painting a floor. Lips that touch latex will never touch mine. Unable to sustain a painterly focus, I usually have to stop at one-point-five coats. Before painting any surface, I attempt to spackle all holes, including the spousely one that first gave voice to the suggestion that I should be painting any surface. Question: If I don't want to get paint all over my hair, skin, and clothes, can I switch from an exterior to an interior paint and let my tissue and organs take the drips? My synonym for "easy clean up" is "inflammable."

That which doesn't kill me means another trip to The Home Depot.

Finish Work: Shticks of the Trades

Dear prospective building trade contractor,

Congratulations! If you're reading this letter, you have successfully completed four of

the five steps I require of all contractors
who wish to be considered for my house
repair work/home improvement jobs. Since
I did not reveal to you beforehand that such
a multi-step process would be part of award-
ing the contract, you may be wondering
exactly what you've (unwittingly!) done
to get this far. Allow me to review your
successful performance to date:

1. After failing to return the $\underline{8}$ phone
messages I left for you about arranging
for an estimate, you did, when I finally
got through to you rather than your
machine, deftly and with no discernable
irony, respond, "Oh, hey, I was just
going to call you."

2. You actually showed up within 10 ten business days of the time we'd specifically
scheduled for you to come by and give me
an estimate.

3. Neither your physical appearance nor
manner of dealing with or eye-balling me
reminded me in any substantive way of
some menacing, psycho John Malkovich or

Christopher Walken movie character, thus I was not overcome with the unsettling, visceral feeling that, through some inadvertent provocation on my part, I would soon have a hammer/wrench/shovel lodged in my skull.

4. Your estimate was written not oral, innocently deceptive not criminally deceptive, upper tropospheric not stratospheric, and, unless I completely misread it, carries a subtext of rage regarding American foreign policy in Central and South America.

The fifth and final step in the job-granting process is the completion of the attached questionnaire. Please answer all the questions as honestly and accurately as the bylaws of your specific trade allow. (Remember, honesty now does not obligate you—legally or otherwise—to such a policy once you're on the job.)

* Are the references you supplied to me not worth the time it will take me to call them or not worth the paper they're written on?

* I understand that you expect 50 percent of the estimate to be paid before you begin the job. Will you accept my dog's personal check?
* When the job doesn't start on time will the delay be indefinite or unknowable?
* At what hourly rate do you bill for "Miller Time"?
* As you're making your endless, loud, banging noises, would it be possible for you to make them in the same 6/8 time as the loud banging noises already going on inside my head?
* You've estimated that this project will require $\underline{5}$ standard eight-hour days. Does your eight-hour day last from 9 A.M. until 3 P.M. or from 9:30 A.M. until 3:00 P.M.?
* On days when you must leave the job in order to get materials, where in the hell are you really going?
* What are the consequences of my hanging around the work area and bringing up topics that give me the opportunity to offhandedly drop terms like, "plumb bob," "bibcock," "monkey wrench," "dado," and "pussy"?
* Will you submit to a Rorschach test where, instead of using the traditional inkblots,

you'll be asked to respond to the oil
stains your truck has left in my driveway?
* Do you swear to keep any and all activities you may witness in my home private
and confidential? Do you further swear
that in the event you fail to fulfill
said promise you will pull down my diaper
and spank me like the nasty, naughty little
girl I am?
* Do you understand that my house is
a nonsmoking house and that failure
to comply with said ban allows me to
seek redress in the form of your slow,
painful, lingering death through emphy-
sema and/or lung cancer or, barring
that, really yellow teeth?
* Will you be tracking your own mud across
my floors and carpets, or am I expected
to provide it?
* If the job turns out to be more serious
and expensive than originally projected,
should I feign surprise?
* Are you willing to forgo legal recourse
in the event that my house is a portal
to Hell?
* When the job doesn't finish on time will the
two of us engage in an ugly, irresolvable

confrontation or will I simply never see, hear from or be able to reach you again?

* When the work has been completed in a less than satisfactory manner, will the reason be that I didn't describe the job properly at the outset, or will you insist that the work "is too" satisfactory?

* For statistical purposes only, would you describe your business ethics as "Gypsy" or "Irish Traveler"?

A final note: Failure to return the completed questionnaire will disqualify you from any further consideration for the job while, admittedly, clearly sending me the message that I can kiss your rosy red ass. Bear in mind, however, that to withdraw and stick it to me now will deprive you of the greater satisfaction of disappearing in the middle of the project and leaving me in the lurch later.

I look forward to hearing from you and to working with you for much longer than any of us anticipates,

Bob Woodiwiss

4} Choosing to Stop Choosing

I freely admit I'm no genius. That fact has been firmly established, over time, by, among other things, educators, standardized tests, my belief in and use of disk jockey endorsed weight-loss products, and my failure to attract an archenemy.

But I'm no idiot, either. Of that, my friends, you can rest assuaged.

So imagine my chagrin when, last week, I had to face the reality that I'm inadequately equipped—acumen-and wisdom-wise—to buy a set of cookware. What's worse, this is only the latest example of my growing incompetence at consumerism. In addition to pots and pans, I also no longer have the stamina or the intellectual wherewithal to buy computer hardware, computer software, electronics, major appliances, car tires, bedding, or any athletic shoe that may actually be used for an athletic activity. Pizza is on the bubble.

What's behind this slowdown in my personal economy? I can tell you in a single word: Choices. Options. Alternatives.

I'm in the housewares department of a major national retailer, i.e., a chain store. (How I wound up shopping at this particular place is not important; suffice it to say, I'd assessed and rank-ordered all the pertinent retailer information available to me via catalogs, the Internet, mass media advertising, and third-party editorial endorsements, taking into consideration details such as breadth of selection, pricing policy, location/s, [including bricks and mortar versus e-tailers], sales associate knowledge, service after the sale, as well as political/social factors [sale of products manufactured in sweatshop, prison, or slave conditions, employee diversity, environmental impact/ contribution to suburban sprawl, active boycotts, predatory marketing practices, particularly objectionable owners and/or lobbying efforts, etc.] and, after several months, randomly picked this place.) My mission: to purchase a full set of evenly heating, lifetime-lasting cookware to replace the stained and streaked, lost-lidded, loose-handled, Teflon-denuded odds-and-ends with which I currently burn my meals. I've done a little research—read some product reviews, talked to some culinarily inclined friends—and I'm relatively confident an up-close, hands-on look and feel will allow me to quickly pull the trigger on this piece of domestic business. I begin the look/feel.

There's non-stick and stick resistant. There's commercial and professional quality. I can buy anodized aluminum, hard-anodized aluminum, stainless steel-clad aluminum, stainless steel-clad copper, all stainless steel, or all copper. Mirror, brushed, or black finish. Any fool, the salesperson seems to indicate, could discern the advantages of each. I imagine concussing him with a nearby display ladle.

Some brands or certain lines within brands have clear lids, some have opaque. Handles come in all-metal, all-metal with heat diffusion design, insulated and wood-sheathed, plus a choice of shapes, including flat, round, or molded hand grip. (Hmm. No self-lifting models. Pity.)

I'm looking for a full set of cookware and I notice one manufacturer has some package deals: eight pieces plus a free omelet pan (a $50 value); a ten-piece on close-out ($90 off); and an eleven-piece on close-out ($75 off) with a free one-quart saucepan (a $60 value) but $40 over my budget. The eight-piece has a fourteen-quart stockpot I'll never use, the ten-piece has three pieces of the same circumference meaning they share a single lid and, therefore, preclude my ability to "cover and simmer" with all three simultaneously, and the eleven-piece, unlike the eight and ten, is commercial grade (better) rather than professional (not bad, but not as good, either). Other brands have similar, though most assuredly not identical, offers.

And, people, I'm simplifying here. Synopsizing. Because not to would produce a work of *Ulysses*ian proportion, Jabberwockian lucidity, not to mention *The Bell Jar*-ian despair.

But this is how it is now. An endless selection of any given product. Each with something extra here, something missing there. Upsides and downsides. Trade-offs and intangibles. "Noncomparable comparables" is how I think of them. The upshot being my old friend and faithful companion "buyer's remorse" has now been replaced by "buyer's paralysis."

Yes, it seems that in corporate America's expanding effort to cover all the bases, cater to all the niches, touch every price point, to upgrade and update products while up-selling and sticking-up purchasers, I no longer have the aplomb to ride-ride-ride the wild surfeit. Instead, I'm drowning in it.

So I'm without cookware. Yet I still need to eat. But rather than try to figure out whether to order from the place offering the two three-item medium pizzas for $12.99 or the one offering the unlimited-items large pizza with a free two-liter Pepsi for $14.99, or the one that'll deliver a large two-topping pizza plus ten hot wings to my door for $13.99, or the six other offers magnet-ed to my refrigerator, I think I'll have a PB&J.

Chocolate-stripe PB.
And seedless raspberry J.
On low-cal sourdough rye.

5} Unhealthy Skepticism

It is my fifth day of pain. My fourth day of discharge. My third day of unwelcome discharge. My second day of painful, unwelcome discharge. The act of standing and walking to the bathroom now seems to require a measure of courage and dedication of purpose that, I humbly suggest, Lance Armstrong or Nelson Mandela might draw inspiration from.

Yet, the inevitable suggestion, when it inevitably comes, comes not from within, but from without. "Go to the doctor," The Partner suggests. Insists. Decrees. And another basic difference between the two of us is revealed: I would rather be surprised by my death; she would rather plan for it.

The waiting room is evenly lit, beige-ly wallpapered. The carpeting suggests an upper-middleclass rec room—indoor/outdoor pile in a bold, unattractive pattern—the better to weather and hide any bodily fluid that is leaked, oozed, or disgorged onto it. The furniture is tasteful, but nondescript, like the food at a national steakhouse chain (though I feel certain my semi-delirium is keeping me from a better simile). Contrary to the familiar jokes, the magazines here—*TIME, Newsweek, Entertainment Weekly, People*—are not years or even months old, but scrupulously current. Though that makes them absolutely no more readable.

The wait is longer than it should be. (Admittedly, the last situation where I found the wait to be of acceptable length was my gestation.) People who have come into the office after me are getting called before me. After twenty minutes, I'm all alone, sitting solo, persistently, painfully—and invisibly!—discharging onto the carpet. It's then that a friendly clipboard with a dour nurse attached appears. "Bob Woodiwiss?" she calls/asks across the desolate waiting room. "I believe that table lamp over there is Bob," I'm tempted to reply. But I don't. Because in my experience caregivers are damned thin-skinned about sarcasm, and it's a foolish person who risks pissing off anyone who may potentially be involved with the administering of one's sigmoidoscopy.

The nurse leads me to a scale. "I need to get your weight," she informs me. Why this is so is a mystery. I'm not here about a weight problem. Or an eating disorder. Or for a physical. Perhaps this is part of some value-added Five Star Service Plan, the equivalent of getting your tires rotated for "free" when you take your car in for $500 worth of new shocks. More likely, it's so she can requisition the right size body bag in which to haul my carcass out of here. Whatever. All I know is, when I get off the scale, my angel of mercy gives me a look that could amputate and says, "Let's try that again. And this time, I need you to stand, not sit."

I'm taken to Exam 4. Where I wait *again*. This time, however, I don't mind. Because once I'm sequestered in an examination room, I like to have a few minutes so I can rifle the cabinets and drawers for interesting and/or useful medical supplies. I find (and pocket) latex gloves (great for painting and caulking), extra-long cotton swabs (ideal for cleaning VCR heads), tongue depressors (there's nothing like them for depressing your friends' tongues) and jumbo gauze pads (which, dripped with a little red food coloring for "blood," make festive Halloween drink coasters).

When I was young and stupid, I felt certain these rummagings would, with persistence, turn up a jackpot of fun, filchible drugs—amyl nitrate poppers, say, or—good God A'mighty!—medical morphine. Now, older and wiser, I realize doctors don't leave narcotics lying around where people like me can get at them. Rather, they write scripts for 'em to people like Elvis.

Long after my pilferage is done, the doctor comes in. Without so much as a "Hello," he begins poking, prodding, tapping, pinching, probing. After about a minute, I interrupt his elaborate self-inspection and ask him if he'll be starting *my* examination soon?

Without answering, he turns to me and raises his eyebrows in a "What seems to be the problem?" manner.

The doctor's unuttered question, his "silent articulation," even through my sickness, sickens me. Isn't it enough that, with increasing frequency, I buy groceries, gas, and sundries, do my banking, check out library books, and conduct innumerable other transactions without the cashier, teller, librarian, or whoever, speaking a single word to me? When, I wonder, did a taciturn look toward the LED's displayed cash total replace the phrase, "That'll be $45.87" or a bartender's wordless finger-point at my empty glass relieve him of the burden of asking, "Can I get you another?" Oh, I admit that, normally, I consider this diminishment of social interaction, human communication, human *connection*, to be at worst right up my alley and at best God's greatest gift, but that's in a retail context, where I'm looking down my nose at a minimum wage worker, not in health care, where I'm at the business end of some well-heeled medico's nose. I want this man to speak to me.

"I'm really sick," I say, letting the phrase hang.

"Yes, I know" he says, out loud, "and you seem to be *physically* ill as well."

OK, then. Now that I feel he's fully engaged, I launch into my checklist of symptoms, including their time of origin and their progress. He nods knowingly, asks a few questions, then proceeds to check my pulse, take my blood pressure, listen to my heart and lungs, peer into my every orifice, etc., etc., etc. Which really pisses me off. Because I know for a fact my HMO won't cover more than one Latin abbreviation per office visit.

I have been seeing the same doctor, this doctor, all my adult life. In that time, I've watched his hairline recede, his waistline expand, his skin sag, wrinkle, and spot, and his ties remain banal. His manner is churlish, occupying some flinty middle ground between David Letterman and Mullah Omar. Working in his favor, however, are the facts that he stays current in his knowledge and he's seen me naked so many times he hardly gasps anymore. Over the years, he's helped me quit drugs, alcohol, and cigarettes, though never all at the same time. I also like it that he doesn't take it personally that I can't remember his name and simply call him "Jocko."

Jocko diagnoses my condition quickly. Even dismissively. He tells me the clinical name for what I have (which sounds, oddly, like the name of a Cuban salsa band), followed by its more common name (which sounds, uncannily, like the name of a Seattle grunge band), and, as he writes it, the brand name of the drug he's prescribing (which sounds, not surprisingly enough, like the single-name name of a New Age singer). He pronounces my condition not serious, not chronic, and easily cured. He leaves before I can ask him to break the bad news to The Partner.

Alone in Exam 4 again, now certifiably not dying, I take solace. And, what the heck, a couple more pairs of latex gloves.

Before leaving the office, I stop at the front desk to take care of my bill. And it is only here, only now, only for this, that *there is no waiting*. None. Because accounts payable is the true energy hub of the modern medical practice. ("Dear Hippocrates: Love the oath. But what say we tweak, 'First, do no harm' to 'First, ascertain co-pay.' Thanks, Ernstopoulis & Youngacles.")

Payment is all efficiency, all smiles, and all major credit cards. Before I know it, I'm processed, paid, fare-thee-well-ed, and, I assume, filed away. Which, today, I tacitly accept. I'm too damn sick to get into a froth about the ironic juxtaposition of *caring* business folk versus *businesslike* caregivers. Maybe tomorrow, if I'm feeling better, I'll just phone in a bomb threat.

6} Party of None

Two phrases are capable of making my right eyelid flutter with the erratic intensity of the wing of a chicken whose neck is being wrung. The first: "I need to check your prostate." (Which, I have to say, I find no less disturbing from medical professionals than from lay persons.) The second: "Let's have a party." In fact, this second phrase—most recently uttered by The Partner—so disturbs me I usually try to deflect it by proposing, "How 'bout you examine my prostate instead?"

> **par·ty:** Derived from the German, "partiereichedammer-ungenhertz," meaning, "Feel free to treat my house with the disregard you usually reserve for a rental car."
> —*The American Heritage Dictionary, 4th edition*

As someone whose self-esteem is woefully dependent on the opinion of others, I find parties are the ultimate in anxiety for me. There are simply too many opportunities to fail, fall short, disappoint. Will a lot of fun people show up or just the losers we know? Are Brie Doritos too pretentious? Is one keg of beer enough? Or will the guests want some, too? Are books-on-tape too conceptual to dance to? Thankfully, The Partner has the answers to all my questions. "Re-fucking-lax, anal boy," she suggests.

> If your party is going to succeed, every detail is an important detail. For example, only after all the shriveled-up rich assholes you invited have RSVPed will you know exactly how many gold-digging whores you'll need to have in attendance. —Martha Stewart

We send out our invitations—some little dealee we designed on the computer. The 3-D font and insipid clip art give it a look that tells invitees, "They designed this little dealee on the computer." Message-wise, our invitation states the party's theme as, "The Fête of a Nation." That was The Partner's clever concept. Personally, I thought if the party had to have a theme, it should be something like, "Swingin' Celebration For People Who Promise They Won't Feed Our Dog Crab Dip or Hot Wings or Brownies or Other Crap But If They Can't Help Themselves and Break That Promise They Swear On Their Mother's Eyes They'll Come Back Tomorrow And Clean Up the Puke." The dog, to my amazement, broke the tie in The Partner's favor.

> Your house should be in perfect order before your first guests arrive. Not so much for their benefit, but because it makes it so much easier to assess the total damage after they leave. —*The State Farm Insurance Good-Time Party Planning Handbook*

The invitation gives a start time of 8:30. Predictably, the first arrivals don't show until 9:30. And the bulk of the crowd—about fifty people—doesn't turn up until 10:30. Meaning this train may not run out of steam until the wee hours. I hold out until midnight, then start trying to drum up interest in my

NyQuil Jell-O Shots. By 1:00 in the morning, feeling desperate, I pull out all the stops and roam the room explaining parliamentary procedure, a topic with proven sleep properties, to random guests. Completely backfiring, an ad hoc quorum forms, declares me "Unfinished Business," and tables me until a party can be held at some future date.

> Fish and Visitors stink after about three seconds when
> Ye are jamm'd into a room full of them.
> —Benjamin Franklin

While I'm timid, awkward, and a social tumor on occasions like this, The Partner is anything but. She is any party's vibrant, bright, warm, magnetic, engaging, easygoing, footloose, and energetic epicenter. She is JFK to my RMN. C3PO to my Hal. Pre-12/18/97 Chris Farley to my post-12/18/97 Chris Farley. Flipper to my fish sticks. I watch her mingle and dance and connect and before long I find myself wishing I had just 1 percent of the vivacity she's got. (I'm currently burdened with 5 percent.)

> Some people are made to circulate. Others to clot and
> cause strokes.   —The Partner

It's 2:40 A.M., and the festivities are still in full swing. The food is holding. The beverages, ditto. A few couples sway NyQuilishly to Michael Crichton's *Airframe* (unabridged). Several guest-clusters have formed, talking, laughing, roaring, discussing every topic under the sun, from the last good movie they saw to the last good movie they heard about. Me, I move invisibly through the tableau, emptying ashtrays, picking up abandoned paper plates, balled-up napkins, and exhausted drinks, avoiding eye contact, silently encouraging the group on the deck pummeling the guy who'd started playing his guitar. I briefly consider going to bed but find I'm in too much fear of the nightmare version of the bad dream I'm living.

> Don't let your hosting responsibilities keep you from enjoying your own party. And don't let the fact that you spend all day, every day in your pajamas hinder your career advancement, either.
>
> —*Hugh Hefner's Guide to Life*

Dawn threatens; the last handful of guests exits, steps out into the damp air. "You do a great party, man," someone says. Oy. That's just what I need. Now, I'll be up until noon trying to decide if he said that ironically or if I just heard it that way.

7} Fishing Buds

We always got an early start. Though, in the interest of full disclosure, I should mention that this was at a time in my life when an early start was anything pre-noon. It was also a time in my life when unemployment was not so much an unfortunate temporary condition as an agreeably unhurried lifestyle. So, on any random weekday from April through October, at some hour, as I say, around midday, Carver and I would load up his Fiat with tackle, plus a couple of rods and reels (or are those tackle, too?), and set out. Wrenching the car in gear, Carver would always announce, "Ready or not, fish, here we come." Again, in the interest of full disclosure, generally speaking, the fish were more than ready.

Carver slips a baggie of buds and some Zig-Zags from the pocket of his flannel shirt and flips them to me. Says I should roll us a joint. Which I do. I pass it to him to fire up. Which he does. Toking and passing, we smoke it to nothingness. Sweet. Perfect, in fact. Because, Jesus, now that we're up and at 'em and out here in the world with these straight-arrow worker bees and their giant fucking American cars and all this goddamn lunchtime traffic, we need something to take the edge off.

I'm not sure how, but Carver knew—and knew how to get to—countless lakes, reservoirs, ponds, rivers, streams, even abandoned, deep-water gravel pits, in which we could try our luck. The only thing these fishing idylls had in common was that they were all located far out in the hinterlands, near crossroad communities like Hicksville and Rube Corners and I Married My First Cousinburg. These were towns where the tonsorial and dental arts still shared a chair and the bait shop was the leading employer. I always felt conspicuous, incongruous in these backwater hamlets where people's teeth were, by my observation, rarer than hen's teeth and varmint was considered "the other white meat." Then again, I was willing to swap with these people my crisp American greenbacks for their Styrofoam cups filled with a scoop of dirt and a few fat worms, so who was smarter than whom?

Carver's twenty-four, about three years older than me. I've known him since I was a senior in high school. Back then, he was dating my older sister, Jody. Now, though, he has a triple role in my life: brother-in-law, best friend, pot dealer. I love how streamlined this is. How simple it makes things. Especially since a lot of the time when I'm buzzed—and thanks to Carver's connections I'm rarely unbuzzed these days—even something like choosing between a Quarter-Pounder and a Quarter-Pounder with Cheese seems epic-ly complex.

We cast our lines. We watched our lines. We smoked our dope and our cigarettes. We coughed much and waited long. As he sat at the water's edge on his campstool, Carver was ever hopeful, endlessly patient, and, as time went on, increasingly competent. Me? I sucked at fishing. And I got worse the longer I kept at it. But this inverted learning curve was fine by me. Because, really, my goal wasn't to put a barbed hook through some bluegill's puckered kisser but to hang out, get high, and zone. So while Carver honestly considered reeling in a fish as a personal triumph over a wily adversary, I saw it as an irrelevant interruption of my right hand's steady, pendulum-like swing between open Doritos bag and open mouth. More analogously put, Carver was Papa Hemingway to my Mama Cass Elliot.

"If you like what we've been smoking, I've got ounces for sale," Carver tells me. If I like it? If I like it? Well, fuck. Let's see. I don't know if it's Septober or Octember; my heart is skipping every fifth beat; my hair is fighting my brain for control of my head; and the shadow across my chest from that tree over there is so heavy I can't stand up. So, come on, Carver, what's not to like?

Occasionally, through the laws of probability, piscine recklessness, and/or the hand of Satan, I would land a fish. And this was not good. Because then I would be compelled, while struggling to unhook the slippery sumbitch and put it back in the water from which I'd just involuntarily dragged it, to gaze into its accusing and desperate eye (yes, "eye;" just try looking a fish in both eyes), and contend with its flailing tail, slick scales and sharp fins, its frantic, gasping gills and convulsively arching body. All as its weak maw pulsed, pulsed, pulsed, open-close, open-close, silently mouthing the question, "Why?…Why?…Why?…Why?…" It took far too many fishing trips for me to realize I'd never ever have a satisfactory answer to give the miserable creature. And not just because I didn't speak "fish."

We do another number on the drive home. It's dark out now. Carver says something about fishing again tomorrow. Fuck a duck. Where does this guy get all his goddamn energy?

I stopped fishing sometime during our second "season" and have never looked back. Carver, still my brother-in-law after some twenty-five years, remains to this day an indefatigable fisherman. (I'm not sure whether indefatigables are a fresh- or salt-water species.) I stuck with dope smoking for several post-fishing years but gave it up when I found drinking could actually take me to the next level: absolute unconsciousness. Carver remains an avid pot smoker (but not a dealer) to this day.

My point? I'm not sure. But it should probably include the word "hooked."

8} Some Days the Bar Eats You

The sign outside is somewhat misleading. It reads Key Club. But this is not a "key club." At least not a key club like, say, the old Playboy Club. Here the word "key" refers to an island, like Key West or Key Biscayne or whatever. And "club" doesn't mean you have to be a dues-paying, card-carrying member to get in; it just means this is a place where you can listen to local live music acts seven nights a week, be overserved cocktails, and sniff around for sex. Here at the Key Club, I like to tell customers, the only restriction to entry is your good judgment.

Inside, the decor is tropical. Island-y. Palm frond thatching here, bright floral print fabric there. A fishing net is draped in irregular droops from the ceiling near the bar; "snagged" in it are cheesy plastic conchs and sand dollars, sad papier-mâché sea horses and starfish. Wide, wood-pier planking gives the floor a dock-like look, and, to complete the illusion, fat three-foot high pilings jut from the floorboards, all linked with thick mooring rope. This Caribbean atmosphere is undermined by the stinging, astringent smell of Pine-Sol—the cleaning crew's disinfectant of choice—which is itself barely holding its own against the indelible odors of stale beer and cigarette smoke. "Dis paradise, mon, it stinks up to da hebbens," I inform the stuffed marlin hanging behind the bar.

* * *

It's a little before 7 P.M. and I'm opening the place. Unlike my environment, I do not look tropical. I look like a bartender in a college bar of declining popularity. All denim and flannel. The way I figure it, with the way business and tips are, the owner should be grateful for every night I come in not wearing lederhosen. Or chewing whale blubber.

Until we open at 7:30, there's plenty to do. First, I have to make as much noise as possible, so that the roaches know something bigger than them has entered their space. This is not so much a warning as a courtesy. Next, I'll stock the bar, cut garnishes, and blender together the sweet, fruity, sticky mixes that'll go in the tropical drinks—Headhunters, Mai Tais, Zombies, Flaming Volcanos, etc.—we specialize in. These drinks take a lot of work up front, but in a few hours when some hot-shit, toss-'em-back frat boy has emptied his wallet on them and is passed out on the bar with his face in a full ashtray, it'll all seem worthwhile.

The waitress, Iris, shows. She's right on theme, sporting a Hawaiian shirt and flip-flops. She's also crying. "I like your shirt," I tell her. (A rule every bartender should live by: Never ask a crying waitress, "What's wrong?") I basically like Iris; she works hard and doesn't do a lot of complaining. In the bar business, that combination in a waitress comes along about as often as a serious beer guzzler who never has to take a piss.

My first customer of the evening is my first customer every evening: Jack. Jack owns a small restaurant across the street and every Monday through Saturday, after the dinner rush, he drifts by the Key Club for a few cocktails. Excuse me—he drifts by the Key Club to get totally, purposefully, and remorselessly shit-faced. Over the past year, I've come to know Jack as a forty-ish, responsible, decent, well-read, good tipping, flaky scalped, rather tedious, long-winded, hopeless alcoholic. He would deny that he's an alcoholic if I were to tell him. And I would tell him if he were a lousier tipper. As it is, he sips his double Manhattans (Jack is not tropical either), smokes his Salems, and pays me to watch him die. Did I mention I went into bartending for the nonstop party atmosphere?

The band starts lugging in its equipment at around 8:30; first set's at 9:00. This is their Friday debut here, but I think it's safe to predict I'll soon be listening to four or five aspiring somebodies performing some guitar-bass-drums rock-related sub-genre at a decibel level which is capable of disrupting the electrical cohesion binding the individual molecules that make up my skull. Because that, my friend, is what a Friday night band in a college bar is. And if you don't know that, you didn't go to college.

9:21. The band's just launched into the first song of their first set. Yes, technically, they should've started twenty-one minutes ago but the clever bastards are taking full advantage of a loophole they've discovered in their agreement. That loophole is the fact that I, the head bartender and de facto person in charge here, don't really give a particular shit if they ever play a chord.

Not caring doesn't mean not benefiting, however. Fact is, I probably benefit more from these guys playing than anyone (unless what we're paying them is how they're able to afford their own apartments, in which case their parents are the primary beneficiaries of tonight's performance). Because from their opening downbeat, extreme volume fills this dinky college bar like a fire hose would fill a shot glass. Instantly. Utterly. Inappropriately. And this ridiculous, assaultive sound reduces my interaction with customers to a delicious minimum. Now, communications are strictly business, drink orders only—concise and shouted, as if the transmissions of a radioman pinned down in a firefight. That means there will be no bitching about classes or work or lovelessness. No confessions. No sports blather. No sincere and meaningless vows or new leaf turnings-over. And I realize for the sixty-third consecutive Friday, that people really aren't so bad if you don't have to listen to them.

Iris, having completed another circuit of the floor and table customers, calls her drink order to me from the waitress station. Mostly, people order beers, GTs, 7/7s. But since the Key Club is a "tropical" bar specializing in "tropical" drinks, there's a steady demand for those, too. (Especially, I suspect, among the "I'm-out-of-refills-on-my-roofies-prescription" set.) The most popular is the Headhunter, an overpriced concoction of three bottom-shelf liquors, two second-rate, syrupy liqueurs, and three fruit juices. These ingredients are then frozen, i.e., blended to an icy slush in a powerful Hamilton Beach. The Headhunter's Slurpee-like quality means drinking them too fast can result in an "ice cream headache." Their too-generous mix of cheap spirits plus refined and natural sugars means no matter what speed you drink them at, come tomorrow morning, you would gladly drain and drink the blood of your family pet if you thought that it could somehow neutralize, however briefly, the several cubic inches of earnest pain you used to know as your head.

* * *

At about midnight, my boss, the owner, Judd, stops by to see how things are going. Judd books all the acts and for him it's all science, no art. Sundays through Tuesdays—deadly, slow nights—he books softer, folkier acts, acoustic solos or duets, people willing to perform for "the door," i.e., the few bucks in cover charges collected from patrons by the doorman, and the opportunity to *reach* and *connect* and *communicate* with five of their friends, a table of off-duty nurses, an adulterous couple who's sure no one they know will see them here, and Jack, my alcoholic regular whose interest in the music might actually increase if he were to go ahead and have one of his blackouts.

On Wednesdays, to lure the desperate party morons who call Wednesday "Humpday," Judd takes things up an energy notch with nonthreatening trios—think Hooty and Two Blowfish—that do lots of covers and'll play for the door, plus a couple free drinks and a minimal cash supplement. Thursday through Saturday, he springs for established, rockin', amply amplified quar-, quin- and sextets, trusting, hoping, betting, they have the loyal and thirsty following that will justify his outlay. Tonight, he appears satisfied with what he sees, crowd/ thirst-wise. Then again, in my experience, bosses are generally satisfied with the things they do themselves. It's we employees who supply them with their many disappointments.

Tips at the Key Club are less than spectacular. I attribute this to the clientele being so young. So unwise and unworldly. Iris has suggested it may have something to do with my attitude, my persona. And Iris doesn't even know I spit in some of the drinks.

* * *

Tonight, as always, four sets of approximately one hour each are played; between sets, the band gets fifteen-minute breaks. These off-stage breathers are important for the musicians to recharge and recenter, that is, to chug down a couple of drinks, duck out the back door for a few quick hits or snorts, arrange a post-show sexual encounter with some improbably star-struck tartlet, jump the shit of a fellow band member for *totally fucking up* some song or other then issuing an empty threat about what'll happen if he does it again, and, if there's time, unstuff their crotches and take a leak. During tonight's last break, the drummer, gin-soaked and over-coked, challenges a table of four jocks to a fight. Thankfully, they don't rise to the bait, which is not surprising since they'd walked out in the middle of the previous set.

The night hits it stride. Blood alcohol levels are in the elusive, idyllic, oh-so-narrow zone that lies between "giddy" and "puke-dribbled chin." The band's fourth and final set is performed furiously, received enthusiastically. The reciprocal energy is uncontainable. Something inexplicable, something potent, something phenomenal is taking place. People and place rock, resound, pound, pulsate as one. Two if you count me.

At 2:10 A.M., the band unplugs, and I give last call. Over the next twenty minutes—closing's at 2:30—I expect the customers who are blind drunk will pair up with the customers who are seeing double and somehow synthesize into creatures of single vision who can then responsibly pilot their cars wherever. And if that scenario seems a little too optimistic, well, that's just who I am.

9} Burning With Passion

It is Sunday. It is sunny. Warm. Today, I will grill the tender flesh of barnyard animals over a fiery bed of crimson coals. I state this not in celebration. Nor do I state it in shame. I state this only to gratuitously goad PETA's prickly membership into a frenzy of outraged letter writing.

Just pre- my teen years, I couldn't get enough of fire. I'd start fires—roaring, tenuously controlled campfires—almost daily in the woods near my house. Once one got going, I'd sit, stock-still, for long stretches. Staring into the flames. Mesmerized. My mind nowhere, empty. Fire was like TV but for a marginally higher denominator.

I lift the lid off my grill with a sudden pop, its edge having been held tight by aged, greasy gunk. This action stirs ash and grit into a low-hanging cloud. I adjust the various soot-gummed vents, scrape the largest of the charred meat crispies and glutinous fat drippings from the black, carbonized grate. And suddenly, the possibility of *E. coli* in the hamburger seems like just one bullet in a loaded gun.

For obvious reasons, I made every effort to keep my pyrothusiasm ("not quite pyromania") secret, but was occasionally found out. Busted. At those times, my parents would rail at and punish me. "What is wrong with you?" Dad would demand. "Do you want to kill yourself?" Mom would ask. Decades later, I'm still working on those tough but fair questions.

Fire time. These days, my preferred method of firing up the charcoal is with a chimney starter, i.e., a tall, steel cylinder that I fill with briquettes, then ignite by lighting some newspapers stuffed into the bottom. The upside of this method is it gets coals going without a noxious petroleum product—like lighter fluid, gasoline, or Dick Cheney's cranial jelly—that can be tasted on the food. The trade-off is that you don't get to repeatedly squirt silvery ropes of hugely flammable juice into smoldering embers and send up monstrously cool, erection-erecting fireballs while intoning phrases like, "I am the Great and Powerful Oz."

At some point, I discovered the very combustible nature of many everyday products, from aerosol deodorant to Brut, NyQuil to hairspray. Flare-ups and flashes and bursts and blasts were now possible. Yow-ee! For such good times, I'd gladly trade the permanent loss of ten pairs of eyebrows.

I arrange an assortment of marinated fare on the grill. Marinades, I'm afraid, have subverted the purity, simplicity, and spontaneity of barbecuing. It's no longer sufficient or acceptable to extemporaneously slap, say, a butterflied pork chop, naked, onto the fire. Rather, it must have first been submerged in a chilled bath of orange juice, Merlot, olive oil, oregano, garlic, turmeric (you've got to get rid of it some place), your choice of at least two but no more than three spices mentioned in a Simon & Garfunkel song, fresh ground pepper, exhausted ground pepper, and the zest of a single caper, for up to forty-eight hours. Oh, to return to the days of the plain and simple, fast and easy, phallic and fat-packed, mysterious and deadly hot dog.

Insects became unfortunate victims of my firebugginess. Caterpillars, moths, spiders, ants, beetles, daddy longlegs, mayflies, all creatures slow enough to be caught and defenseless enough to not sting, bite, spray, or otherwise meaningfully resist were consigned to the flames without regard or regret. Looking back, I can't help thinking that if the Sixth Commandment is meant as an all-inclusive, black-and-white kind of thing, I'm one hopelessly screwed son of a bitch.

To barbecue well takes knowledge and control. Steaks should be grilled at a higher temperature than shrimp. Leg of lamb requires more time per side than leg of hummingbird. Porto-bello mushrooms, bell peppers, and tofu must always be "accidentally" flipped down into the coals where vegetables belong. And, guys, remember, when you put on that special barbecue apron you got for Father's Day, you really don't qualify as a guy anymore.

I stopped making fires in the woods the day Dad decided I was old enough to make them for him in the grill. This had nothing to do with the trust and responsibility he was showing me and everything to do with the fact that I now realized building fires was work and should be avoided at all costs.

Later, long after dinner has been eaten and cleaned up, I notice I smell like fire. Like smoke and charcoal and meat. This scent, it occurs to me, would make a good cologne. Maybe call it *Eau de Feu.* Or Twelve-Year-Old Boy's Obsession.

10 } Black-and-White Whine

"Can I see your license?"

I get that question a lot. Partly because it's the start of my favorite sexual role-playing game, Naughty Out-of-Season Bonefisher Happened Upon by Unmerciful Game Warden-ess. But in this instance, it's because a cop has me pulled over and is initiating the traffic citation sequence. He is pear-shaped to the stereotypical extreme, an officer who, in the event of a foot chase, could be outpaced by any suspect fleeter than a walking catfish. I know that from here on out any mention of the word "donut," regardless of context, will result in blows to my kidneys.

I've been ticketed many, many times in my driving career. Mostly for speeding. A few for running red lights and stop signs. Two for driving under the influence of Brian Wilson's psychiatrist. At one point, the critical mass of my violations cost me my driving privileges for a full year. Worse, when I got them back, it cost me big money, as my insurance company informed me I'd been rerated and would now be paying the same premiums as "a drunk six-year-old male resident of metro Detroit driving a new Jaguar with 'iffy' brakes."

As the cop looks at my license, I can sense he's ready to begin my most hated part of the ticketing process: the rhetorical quiz. "Do you know why I stopped you?" "Do you know how fast you were going?" "Are you in a hurry?" "Do you know what the speed limit is on this road?" "If this traffic stop were taking place across the International Dateline would you be in trouble yesterday or not until tomorrow?" As always, I volunteer to be maced if we can skip right to the "running my plates" part.

The first few times I was pulled over, I was very polite with the officer. I agreed a lot—something I almost never do in "real life." I ended sentences with, "sir," and "ma'am," often correctly matching it to the sex of the officer. I went the extra mile, not only keeping my hands where they could be seen, but employing them in an entertaining "trapped in a box" mime routine, as well. I even resisted asking if, based on Kent McCord's and Martin Milner's portrayals on Adam-12, *I should assume all uniform cops are closet homosexuals. All this niceness, I figured, might dissuade the cop from writing the ticket. It never did. Discouraged, I became terse and dour in my dealings with law enforcement. And judging from the countless austere, unsmiling mug shots I see on the nightly news, I am not alone in that practice.*

He's checking for wants and warrants, a process that by comparison makes continental drift seem frenzied. I sit in my car, the cruiser behind me, its lights flashing, time frozen. I feel so conspicuous. So busted. I look at the drivers zipping by. They turn to look at me—me, the vehicular miscreant—and shake their heads, condemning my pathetic example. *Vroom,* there goes my kindergarten teacher. *Vroom,* and my old boy scout leader. *Vroom,* I'm pretty sure *that* was Jesus. *Whizz,* and god*damn* if it isn't that one self-righteous bastard in every town who's always riding around on his recumbent bike.

There have been instances over the past couple years, where I'll be "making good time" (a euphemism I like because it makes speeding sound like a conscientious business practice) and suddenly—too late!—I'll see a cop with his radar gun pointing right at me. I drive on, of course, backing off the gas just enough to get legal, and, for the next minute or two, checkcheckcheck the rearview, waiting for the flashing lights to explode on, to start gaining on me. But they don't. Prompting me to throw my head back in a mocking laugh. Then, because this reaction is so hopelessly clichéd, I snort derisively at myself. The predictability of which triggers a dismissive chortle. Begetting a scornful sneer. Etc. And before long, I come to the realization that cops are the least of my problems.

"I clocked you doing fifty-seven in a thirty-five mile per hour zone," I'm informed. The officer pushes the ticket toward me, instructs me to sign, then hands me my copy along with a fine schedule (that's "fine" as in dollar amount to pay, not "fine" with a connotation of excellent graphic design and quality paper stock). Now, as I mentioned, these days I adopt a terse and dour attitude in these situations. Not smart, not feisty. I know responses like, "You really blew it, Columbo, I don't fit any of the racial profiles your force is currently persecuting" or "Thanks to you, I'll never make it home before the PCP kicks in" will not serve me well with my badged-and-blue persecutor. Instead, "Um-hmm," is all I say. Before I can merge back into traffic, though, it occurs to me what a thankless job this nation's police officers have. With that in mind, I back up to where my cop is standing so he can thank me for giving him and his buddies something to do.

11 } Seven Stray Days in May

1.

We sidle halfway into the row. It's the bottom of the first, two outs. No one's happy about the timing of our arrival. Understandably. After all, our passing blocks each person's view for 0.8 seconds and a game is *only* ten or twelve thousand seconds long. Sor-ry.

I'm carrying a hot dog and a beer; my nephew, Glenn, has opted for the crabcakes and a Long Island iced tea. Later, when he launches into his recurring lament about player salaries wrecking the game, I'll have to inform him that, personally, I believe his choice of ballpark refreshments (not to mention their availability) constitute a greater threat to the traditions of our National Pastime than if the infield grass were to be replaced with Saltillo tile.

He'll balk. Roll his eyes. Argue. Because Glenn's grown up with a different game than I did. The DH, three divisions, wild card teams, the World Series wrapping up around College Bowl season, he's fine with that stuff. The screwy kid. One thing's for sure, though: by game's end, none of that crap'll matter and we'll be jawboning about the one subject all true baseball fans agree on: Bob Costas's tongue must be cut from his mouth and fed to an undiscerning dog.

2.

There's a tornado warning in effect until 8 P.M. (A tornado

warning means conditions are right for frequent program interruptions by fear-mongering meteorologists repeatedly cautioning us of *the potential for* certain doom.) Lightning cracks. Thunder explodes. The house rattles and shivers. The dog trembles, looks to me with uncomprehending eyes. To this beast I am God, and at this moment he clearly expects me to do something Godlike. Pointing toward the fulminating heavens, I shout, "That, vile cur, is for the humping of My Leg last night."

What can I say? I'm an Old Testament kind of God.

3.

Dinner alfresco. How continental.

Many of our surrounding diners are cigarette smokers. How very continental.

Our waiter is indifferent, rude, and largely invisible. Continental? *Mais oui.*

The petite portions are a red cape waved in front of the snorting bull that is my appetite, yet the prices are staggering. *C'est trés, trés continental, aussi.*

We dine and dash. U-S-A! U-S-A! U-S-A!

4.

This perfect day was made for a convertible. Not owning one, I head to my nearest BMW dealership. There, I ask to test drive a new Z8 roadster. The salesman, either familiar with this ploy or distrustful of a customer clad only in a Speedo, flatly refuses my request. To my surprise, however, he offers to hold a photograph of the car in front of me while blowing briskly into my face and hair. The experience is immeasurably enhanced by his breath having that new car smell.

5.

I grab a soda from deep, deep down in the sweaty, ice-packed, galvanized tub. I sharply blow the clinging, frosty chips off the can top, then pop it, *phttt*. The cola's cold is vicious; the carbonation stings my throat with needles of painful refreshment. Oh-h-h, yeah. Picnics are *so* fine!

Over there, in the meadow, a Frisbee makes slicing sorties over butterfly airspace. The sweet slap of ball on mitt and bright clang of well-aimed horseshoes add rhythm to myriad birdsong, creating a fantasia *en plein air.*

Soon, gathered children will glow orange, faces reflecting a campfire's toasting embers. Chaste marshmallows will be violated by whittle-tipped sticks and plunged into the purifying inferno, while the scent of burnt sugar mingles with pine smoke to paint the languid air of creeping darkness…

"Umm, babe, don't let me have any more of those brownies from the 'adult' pan."

6.

I pour a splash more coffee and look out the kitchen window at the backyard. The lawn needs cutting. The lawn needs fertilizing. The lawn needs weeding. And seeding. And aerating. Watering. Thatching. Edging. Jesus. (That last is an expression of disbelief; my lawn doesn't need Jesus. Probably.)

I upend my cup in the sink. Time to get to it. Have at it. I want this kitchen window boarded over by noon.

7.

Mom's ready to go to the cemetery. Make that cemeteries, plural. Her folks are in one; her grandparents are in another; her sister's in a third. This is the same circuit Dad used to call the

"Ritual Memorial Day Tour." Of course, that was before Dad became "Tour Stop #4." In the years since I took over as wheelman, I've rechristened it, "Mom's (End-Of-The-)Road Show."

Graveside at the last cemetery, after nearly one hundred miles of driving and the whole day gone, it occurs to me what a lousy, stupid, pointless holiday this is. Visiting the *dead*. As if *they* care. I decide then and there that my time on this planet would be much better spent lavishing more attention, more care, more love, on the living. To facilitate my complete embrace of this tender notion, I make an unscheduled stop at a nearby kennel and trade Mom for a puppy.

12} No, Please, Eat *Me.*

2863 Mencken St.
Cincinnati, OH 45232
June 21, 2004

To: My Expectant Hosts,

Your dinner invitation for next Saturday evening is very generous and greatly appreciated, but I will be unable to join you and your other guests for one or more of the following reasons:

a. I am a shy, solitary person who prefers to remain cloistered in the quiet and isolation of his Sanctum Sanctorum—now with DirecTV. For future reference, you should be aware that it is only because I am, on occasion, compelled to leave the house—to work or attend school or pick up my newspaper off the lawn or obtain a controlled substance—that I ever made your unsought acquaintance in the first place, and I'm now begging you to leave me the hell alone.

b. You live in the suburbs, Mr. and Ms.
Weed & Feed, and my sense of adventure
doesn't include exposing myself to the
toxic allergens and rabid opossums, the
overblown barbecue bonhomie and overall
aesthetic stasis of your stultifying
bricks-and-vinyl-siding prefabricated
nightmare. But thanks so much for
thinking of me.

c. Having eaten nearly 5,000 consecutive
identical meals (half a Sara Lee Cheesecake and two twelve-ounce cans of Mountain
Dew, followed by, for dessert, half a
Sara Lee Cheesecake) since June 19, 1987,
I am over halfway to making the Guinness
Book of World Records in the Consecutive
Identical Meals (Packaged/ Processed
Foods) Category. Since I doubt that this
is your intended meal plan and since,
if you were to decide to serve this menu,
I would feel that you were mocking or
patronizing me, which would ruin my
appetite and therefore negate the purpose
of having any dinner at all, I will, of
necessity, be dining at home that evening.

d. I swore the last time I was around
your child/ren that the next time I was
around your child/ren I would indulge my

urge to kick the life out of his/her/
their aggravating, unmanageable, and
unmanaged ass/es.

e. You have odd hair and I feel
uncomfortable around it.

f. Your home is not handicap accessible.
And while, yes, I realize that I am in no
way physically handicapped, it's the goddamned principle of the thing. Besides,
what if I were to become handicapped
while at your house for dinner? How would
I get out? (And believe me, if I became
paralyzed or crippled or was otherwise
stricken at your home, I'd be plenty
pissed about it and would want to leave
immediately.) Thanks but no thanks.

g. Your lifestyle makes me feel totally
inadequate/too materialistic. If only you
had more/less stuff. Jetted/drove to
more/fewer vacation spots closer to/far-
ther from home. Dressed with some measure
of style and taste, you Gap-draped
drone/Stopped flaunting the fancy-shmancy
designer labels, for Christ's sake. And
what's with your car? A ride like that
really sends a message about who you are
and how you see yourself, and clearly,

we're from different worlds. Until we're closer in income and core values (who knows, in the coming years our lives might converge when you're on the way up/down and, conversely, I'm on the way down/up) I think it's best we not break enriched white bread/rosemary-olive focaccia together.

h. One or more of those around the dinner table is sure to have voted for The Politician Formerly Known as Governor Bush (he is not the President). This indicates a level of mental acuity that can only mean I'll spend most of my evening cutting up their meat for them, a duty I respectfully pre-decline.

i. Have you forgotten you once tried to kill me?

j. I will be out of town leading the other half of my double life, and that life's wife and I are going to a dinner party with people I respect too much to even think about declining their generous offer. Ah, well, I suppose conflicts like this are to be expected.

* * *

I hope you understand that I am entirely
unwilling to take the time and far
too indifferent to make the effort to
indicate which explanation applies to
your invitation specifically. So please
choose whichever ones reinforce your
existing notions about yourself and/or
me and accept my impersonal regrets.

Explanatorily,

Bob

13 } Let's Put Christ Back in "Christ, I Hate the Holidays": A Yuletide Triptych

Smells Like Christmas Spirit

The holiday season is rife with rich, powerfully evocative smells. For instance, I just this moment become aware of a sharp scent of evergreen wafting through the house, into my office. And even though I know it's only Myrna, the cleaning woman, downstairs huffing Pine-Sol spray again, I can't help but be reminded of the long-ago Christmases of my youth.

Back in those days, on Christmas Eve, Dad would heft an axe onto his shoulder, and together he and I would trek through the woods that abutted our subdivision, looking for the perfect tree, i.e., any species of evergreen, less that eight feet tall and out of sight of the landowner's house. I couldn't tell you whether it was skillful hunting or good fortune, but, somehow, we always found what we were after. When we did, a spray of fragrant wood chips and strong profanity would fill the air as Dad crudely hacked the quivering pine to the frozen ground. Sweaty but satisfied, he'd start toward home dragging the coniferous carcass behind him, leaving me with the instruction to "make it look like suicide."

Later, at home, Mom, my sisters, and I would decorate the tree while Grandma sat on the couch filling the room with a heady bouquet of bourbon fumes and Chesterfield smoke. To this day, whenever I walk into a stuffy, unventilated dive of a bar and take in a nose full of the room, I can almost hear Grandma's frail slur and her annual recitation of Clement

Moore's "That's the Ugliest *Fucking* Tree I've Ever Seen in My *Fucking* Life."

Come Christmas morning, a warm, reassuring aroma would seep through the house: waffles. Or, more accurately, waffles and melting polymer fibers. Somehow, every year Mom's half-size-too-big Eva Gabor wig would tumble from her head only to get caught in the hot jaws of the waffle iron. I swear, if it weren't for the inconsolable sobbing and gratuitous dog kicking, you'd think she did it on purpose.

After breakfast it was time to open our gifts. Dad would always get a bottle of Old Spice. Like an incorrigible little kid, he'd insist on uncapping the bottle right away, unleashing the balmy fragrance of nonthreatening machismo. Also like a little kid, he'd invariably splash on far, far too much of the bracing aftershave. We could tell it was too much because, moments later, when he'd light up his next Lucky Strike, his head would go up in flames and, after putting him out, we'd have to rush him to the ER.

By the time we'd get back, the house would be filled with the smells of roast turkey, dressing, mashed potatoes, and fresh-baked rolls. This told me that Uncle Lionel, a large man of unusually high metabolism and a liberal applier of Holiday Feast Scent RightGuard, had arrived. Mom, meanwhile, would be in the kitchen cooking up the traditional German Christmas dinner: braised knucklebone stuffed with headcheese. It was then I'd find my way to the bathroom for some traditional pre-puking.

After dinner, Dad would get out the camera, and soon the flash bulbs were popping, sizzling, smoldering. Dad, it must be said, was a dreadful, indiscriminate photographer with a cruel knack for capturing the wrong moment, for provoking the worst in a subject. He didn't so much steal your soul with a photo as rob you of your humanity. In high school, I was able to keep myself in beer money by selling my family pictures as production stills from snuff films.

But perhaps the most distinctive yuletide fragrance from my youth was the one that came late in the day. It was then that the dog, hours after being surreptitiously fed rich holiday foods under the table and, once the table was cleared, openly given a hearty helping of greasy scraps in his bowl, bloated and gassy, would begin farting. Uncle Lionel, in an effort to mask these foul emissions, would light the scented candle in Mom's Christmas centerpiece. Before long, the air would be redolent with a mixture of flatulence and cinnamon. A peculiar, disconcerting, impossible-to-ignore synthesis that, for some reason, I'm reminded of every time I see Michael Douglas and Catherine Zeta-Jones.

At any rate, sometime around midnight, all-in and yawning, I'd climb the stairs, ready for bed. The big day was over. Gone far more quickly than it had come. But I really didn't mind. Because I knew that come next year, the holidays would smell again.

Lap Dunce

If someone were ever to utter in my good ear the familiar bit of treacle, "It's always darkest just before the dawn," I'm afraid I'd have to insist that, like cocktail hour, it's always "just before the dawn" somewhere in the world. Similarly, what the average person would designate a frisky litter of snuggly puppies, I would call a swarming maelstrom of the unwormed. And, on difficult days, days when I'm in great need of hope and relief, I like to make a mental escape to the lush swelter of the tropics. Specifically, Jonestown. More specifically, in 1978.

I mention these sullen tidbits not to inspire pharmaceutical conglomerates to rush to market an SSRI the size of a hockey puck, but to establish the utter preposterousness of my ever taking on the role of Santa Claus, the purported "jolly old elf." Yet, at one time, a woman I was deeply involved with, a woman assigned to manage a desperately short-handed Santa's Wonderland Workshop and Lap Sittery in a local mall, implored me, as a favor, to do just that. And I, solely out of love, accepted. If there are any tender youths out there, I beseech you to recognize and digest this powerful argument against ever, ever falling in love. At least, with someone in management.

The suit, I can tell you, is not for the faint of heart. By the time I'd arrive at the mall for my evening shift, the unbreathing scarlet polyester-velvet costume had been heavily sweated in by a sequence of minimum wage zeroes ("zeroes" because they'd taken this gig not, like me, out of love, but—sweet suffering Christ!—to pay their rent). The stomach padding was fetid and disgusting, with a look, smell, and feel that emptied my brain of all words except "flophouse pillow." And despite an occasional dry-cleaning, the suit's exterior was, when looked at closely, a virtual tapestry of children's oozings, emissions, excretions, droppings, and expectorations—the residue of Fruit Roll-Up drool here, evidence of a poorly fitted Huggie there. To be enrobed in this oh-so-festive holiday garment was to be surrounded by a greater number of DNA samples than the most overworked crime lab technician.

As for the long, white wig, beard, and moustache—items made of (I swear) un-dry-clean-able, bleached yak hair—I can only marvel that I've lived to tell the tale. It was an ugly, obvious fact that the errant hairs constantly migrating into my mouth had, just hours or minutes earlier, migrated into the foul, dank, mossy, never-flossed maws of my co-Santas. Or, worse, had been in the rude grasp of a four-year old germ magnet, some unwitting carrier of pink eye or lupus or cholera or penis dropoffidus. Why, I'd have been at less risk sipping raw, unrefrigerated oysters from a rented bowling shoe.

Don't think because Santa is the beloved benefactor of all the world's children (Jews, Muslims, Buddhists, Deists, Druids, Atheists, etcetera, excluded, of course) that he operates with any great license. Hardly. Before I assumed the Santa throne for the first time, a mall flunky handed me a comprehensive code of behavior to read and sign. As I recall, the three strongest warnings contained in this document were: 1. Do *not* greet children with "Ho-ho-ho;" it will frighten and traumatize them. 2. To avoid allegations of impropriety or molestation, do *not* lift the children onto your lap; let them climb or be placed there. 3. After a child tells you what s/he wants for Christmas *remain non-committal.* Do *not* promise or indicate *in any way* that s/he can expect to get what s/he's asked for.

As I signed along the dotted, I couldn't help but wonder what, in light of these constraints, I was going to bring to a child's Christmas experience that a Santa sculpted from a large, hard, imported cheese couldn't just as easily supply.

Each shift, before the first supplicant of the evening approached, I'd gaze out over a serpentine waiting-line that looked absolutely endless. Once the polyester-velvet rope fell, however, and the line started moving, that changed.

Then it *felt* endless. So much so, I began to suspect that, after taking leave of my lap, the children were stealing off to a secret location, putting on *Mission: Impossible*/Martin Landau-quality, full-face latex masks and racing back into line for another go at Saint Gift Boy. Which, when I thought about it, went a long way toward explaining The Code's Rule #4: Do not attempt to rip the face off of any child. Of course, I eventually figured out that I was wrong, that none of the children were actually wearing *Mission: Impossible*/Martin Landau-quality full-face latex masks. Which, I assure you, didn't make Rule #4 one iota easier to obey.

Santa's actual work duties are pretty boilerplate: Hold child. Listen to child. Send child on merry way. And that's fine. Because, it turns out, Santa's visitors are fairly boilerplate, too. In all my weeks of being a "little people" person, my lap was occupied by no more than four basic types. (I'm not talking about your child/ren, reader. Of course, *your* child/ren is/are absolutely unique and the refreshing exception to every rule.) These types, in descending proportions, are:

1. **Wieners.** These kids recognize that in order to get what they want for Christmas they've got to go through Santa. Unfortunately, Wieners use every last shred of their nerve to simply *approach* The Bearded One. Once in his presence, they cannot muster *a single audible word.* The child's whole visit is comprised of looking at the ground, rubbing his/her face and failing to respond to a throne-side parent who repeatedly caws, "Tell him, (child's name). Tell Santa what you want." I figured my role was to say helpful things, like, "Spit it

out, goober, or I'll take back last year's toys," and "Have you thought about taking a Dale Carnegie course?"

2. **Gimmees.** Typically, a kid head-to-toe in branded/licensed clothes (Gap, L.L. Bean, Oshkosh, Sesame Street, Pooh, Mickey, etc.) bearing a long, unambiguous and prioritized wish list. I had several kids bring in catalog pages, either to make their presentation more compelling (kind of kiddie "overheads") or to ensure Santa, old feeb that he is, doesn't screw up (you know, like *last* year when there was an *Endocrinologist* Barbie under the tree instead of a *Gastroenterologist* Barbie). Less a "visit" than a "transaction."

3. **Wailers.** These stricken, fearful children are forced to sit on Santa's lap by parents who, apparently, believe this is a season of tears, shrieks, spasmodic writhing, and struggle to flight. Such emotional distress, such blind terror, is rarely seen—or inflicted—in public. Glad I could help.

4. **Goofettes.** High school girls (in pairs, sporting braces, school jackets, no boyfriends) and women over forty (one at a time, too much jewelry, too much make-up, too much hair) who think it's cute to bust Santa's sweaty, underpaid, captive chops. Lots of giggling from the former, lots of sexual innuendo from the latter ("Yes, Madame, that is a candy cane in Santa's pocket, and, no, I'm not at all glad to see you.").

***

My weeks *en rouge* were both physically and psychologically debilitating. Physically, because I spent hours on end sitting on a too-short, rigid plywood throne in a too-heated mall dressed in a too-polyester velvet suit, gloves, boots, thick, insulating, poly-foam "fat," a long wig, and mask of facial hair while attempting to contain on my lap the veritable formicary of children that one-by-one paraded there, each wriggling and wrenching and squirming and pulling and punching and poking and plunging to a different drummer. Which may not qualify as Herculean or Sisyphusian, but is surely Pilatean, if not Bowflexian.

As for my psychological trauma, it was twofold. First, as an avowed atheist, I felt I was betraying my principles by portraying a religious figure, i.e., a "saint." Only much later did I discover that by denying God, I had tremendous wiggle room on principles. Second, I found myself in a continuous struggle to reconcile this internal conflict: If I loved the woman in charge of this Wonderland so much that I allowed myself to be shanghaied *into* the job, why did I, while *on* the job, cling to the reparatory image of her severed head being baked like an apple in a convection oven? Moreover, how, exactly, should I interpret its cinnamon-sugar glaze?

It didn't take long to realize that the real reason Santa takes up residency in America's malls isn't to provide fond memories to tykes flushed with excitement; it's to sell eight-by-ten memories to parents flush with coin. And so, as each visit wrapped up, an elf, standing behind a camera six feet away, would try to coax a salable look and smile from me and *die Kinder*. To get the money shot, these elves, i.e., cute young women dressed in peppermint-striped tights and shorty-short green holly-scalloped tunics, would coo, cajole, entice, pucker, clap, flutter, wave, dance, spin, sway, and undulate. By the time an elf's full routine had been performed, I was not only smiling, I was on the brink of shouting "Grind it, baby," and tucking a $20 bill in the waist of her tights. So much for my ability to distinguish naughty from nice.

At the end of each shift, Santa had to make his way back to the changing room (which was the mall office, the same out-of-the-way place from whence rent-a-cops spring, shop-lifters are detained, and public johns abut) and his street clothes. This meant a long walk through the mall, smiling at and waving to the throngs of holiday shoppers along the way. Adults smiled and waved back, called "Hello, Santa." Children pointed and beamed. To me, it was this interlude that felt the most like Christmas. Because the world seemed joyous and hopeful and generous of spirit. And I could just keep moving.

My engagement at the "North Pole" was spread over about three weeks; altogether, I was scheduled for twelve shifts and I worked twelve. In my countless hours on the throne, I held every child who would allow it, regardless of age, mood, 'tude, or substance spewed. I smiled for and into the flash camera whenever prompted and, by December 24th the spots before my eyes were so familiar I'd given all of them names. And while, no, I wasn't the jolliest St. Nick, or the second jolliest, or even the second-least jolliest, there were no charges brought, lawsuits threatened, or vendettas sworn, either.

The last time I put on the appalling Santa suit and its accoutrements was on Christmas Eve. Since the manager—the woman who'd drafted me into the Red-with-White-Trim Army in the first place, the woman I loved—had to close things up that day, I agreed to work, too. The mall closed at 5 P.M., but, from lunchtime on, my lap had zero traffic; the final hours of the final day of Christmas shopping are not about innocent, wide-eyed children but desperate, impulsive adult men. Santa's Wonderland stood as a shunned, unvisited, and lonely island—Cuba with pine-rope and cotton-batting snow.

After this final shift, as I changed into my street clothes in the mall office, my paramour came in, limp from exhaustion and relief. She thanked God it was all over. She said she owed me hugely for helping her out, for coming through for her. She crossed the room to where I sat, leaned over, and kissed me on the lips. I pulled her down onto my lap. Where, it was beginning to seem, everyone belonged.

Decor Meltdown

They look innocent enough. Or at least benign. They bear no skulls and crossbones. No warnings from the Surgeon General. No HazMat symbols. Yet, from vast past experience, I know that what's inside these nondescript containers will, by the end of the day, have me moaning in pain, begging to be put out of my misery. Because what's inside—and soon to be outside—these boxes and bins are the hellish embellishments of the season, that is, Christmas decorations. I survey them. Assess them. Grok them. A bile tasting of candy cane rises in my gullet.

What is it about these hackneyed gimcracks and over-bright gewgaws, this yuletide frippery and festoonery, that so brings me down? Is it the forced clutterization of a normally restrained and ordered home decor? Is it the cheesy Christmas music that comes out of everything from the *Ernest Saves Christmas* windup snowglobe to smiling Frosty the Snowman's circularly perforated and miniaturely be-speakered ass? Is it the introduction of angels and Saint Nick and Baby Jesus, et al, into the household of a man (me!) who considers even the most ambivalent Unitarian a foot-soldier of fascistic religiosity? Is it the sheer physical labor of hauling boxes, rearranging furniture, ladder climbing, garland stringing, tree erection, tinseling the untinseled, gingerbreading the ungingerbreaded, aerosol snowing the tinsel and gingerbread, riveting prosthetic antlers onto the dog's head, etc.? Is it the knowledge that I'll be performing this excessive, annoying process precisely in reverse mere weeks from now? Is it The Partner's willingness to brandish in my direction a heartbreakingly tender expression of hope, expectancy, and trust in order to gain my cooperation in this totally abhorrent operation? I don't know. I really haven't given it any thought.

The first and biggest job is stringing the outdoor lights. For this I'll need to use an extension ladder (or, as they're called by the Texas Department of Corrections, "lethal injection's cheaper alternative"). As both an inept and a coward, I always put safety first when using a ladder, meaning I climb it in painfully slow, tremulous steps, then, while clinging desperately onto the gutter with one hand, I impotently flail at the work with the other. After two to three hours of this I declare the job finished, timidly climb down and tell The Partner I decided against her proposed traditional edging of the windows and eaves in favor of a more conceptual, Jackson Pollock-esque "Action Lighting" approach.

* * *

"Let's put the dancing Santa on the coffee table," The Partner says. "That's a wonderful idea," I want to say, "you've found the perfect place for it." But of course, I can't say it. I'm not that good an actor. And the blatant insincerity of my remark would trigger a long, silent winter of sexlessness or, worse, a long talky winter of couple's counseling. "OK," is the best response I can make and I make it. "Hmm, I don't know," she says seriously, as if the proper placement of this hip-twisting piece of bearded crap is what will land us a spread in next month's *Architectural Digest.* "Maybe it should go on the mantel." What, I think, and give it an additional three feet in which to gain momentum and shattering speed in the event of an unfortunate topple? "That's a wonderful idea," I respond without a trace of thespianism, "you've found the perfect place for it."

Up goes the garland. Up go the stockings. Up goes the pine-scented plastic wreath. Up goes the sleigh-reindeer-*USS Enterprise* mobile. Up goes the ceramic crèche with the three-legged camel and the pirate Weeble in the manger filling in for the long-missing Christ child. Up comes my lunch.

Finally, it's tree-trimming time. As is tradition, we've bought the tree with the sharpest, driest needles on the lot so that, as I attach the light strands to the inner boughs, my arms get more heavily scored than a touching moment in a Spielberg film. Once I've finished with the lights, the ornaments can be hung. The unfortunate fact here is that while The Partner's ornament collection grows with every passing year, the size of our tree, for space reasons, has remained relatively constant. This means that by the time all her various bulbs, balls, bells, stars, and figures are in place, the burdened limbs strain earth-

14 } Teacher's Putz

Think back.

You're in sixth grade. The topic of the moment is, oh, I don't know…transportation. The teacher says, "I want you to think about all the cars and trucks and trains and airplanes that you see everyday. Now what is it that makes them go? What do you have to put in a car so the engine will run…?" She pauses rhetorically. "Gasoline and oil, that's right. All right, now, think about this: what would happen if there were no more gas and oil? If we ran out. We'd still have to get ourselves and other things from place to place, wouldn't we? But how? What new kind of transportation might be invented? Something that wouldn't need gas? Let's use our imaginations. We'll go around the room, starting with Barry…"

Ah, Barry. You remember ol' Bare, don'tcha? Nice enough guy but with all the imagination of a bald tire. Likely to give a response along the lines of, "A super no-gas truck" or, if he's particularly inspired, "A magic truck." The glorious, predictable, brain-dead bastard! Yes, glorious. Because Barry is absolutely incapable of coming up with, "Anti-gravitational thermo-bubble with electrogyroscopic auto-impulse thrusters," the nifty answer that, quite unexpectedly and uncharacteristically, has popped into your noggin, a creation cobbled from comic book artwork, sci-fi movies, some incidental reportage you picked up off a stupid *National Geographic* special thing your Dad was watching on TV one night that you couldn't coerce him to click off of for something decent, and intuitive crappàge. And by leaving *your* answer—your *brilliant* answer—to you, Barry has proved himself a true friend, though not the kind you have to talk to or do stuff with.

But just because Barry doesn't "steal" your answer, that doesn't mean you're out of the woods, anti-gravitational thermo-bubble-wise. Not by a long shot. There are twenty-seven other kids between Barry (last name Aaron or Abbott or Alexander), sitting in the right front corner of the teacher's seating plan, and you (your last name starting with W, X, Y, or Z), in the rear left. Twenty-seven potentially double-crossing classmates who, through pure dumb luck and/or crisis-induced telepathic channeling, might blurt out the exact idea you have in mind and leave you answerless. The classroom/academic equivalent of stopping a tetherball with your wiener.

Okay. Maybe not the *exact* idea. But one of them—number six or fifteen or twenty-two—could definitely conceivably vaguely propose, "A floating thing…that people could, like, ride in…?" which could definitely conceivably move the teacher to probe, "And what do you think that would look like?"

This line of questioning makes you highly anxious. Apprehensive. Incredulous. You tell yourself, *This* isn't *happening. I* can't be *witnessing a teacher aiding and abetting some delinquent weinerhead in the commission of Grand Theft: Answer.*

Lord almighty. You feel flushed. Helpless. There you are, stuck in the left rear corner of the room with no recourse. The innocent victim of alphabetical order. You begin to silently chant, "Don't say 'bubble'…Don't say 'bubble'… Don't say 'bubble'…" whereupon your flailing, still-under-the-gun classmate offers, "It'd be…round? Like a ball?" Yes! "Or… maybe clear." Fuck! "Like a bubble?" Fuckfuckfuckfuckfuck.

That stumbling, grasping little shit. S/he did it. S/he stole your answer. Or at the very least terminally tainted it by getting a critical part of it out into the air first. The answer that, had you been permitted to present it, fresh and in full, with some modicum of confidence and clarity (two traits neither number six nor fifteen nor twenty-two has *ever* exhibited and you've know all three since kindergarten, when they were chronic paste eaters), would have produced a hushed awe in the classroom and forced everyone to reevaluate their assessment of you, to view you as existent rather than nonexistent, to consider your haircut not so much "tragic" as "eccentric."

Now, instead, your response lays dead in your brainpan, unspoken, unspeakable, prekilled, a soldier choked to death on a chicken bone the day before being called up to the warfront.

So you sit there, bummed, waiting, listening. Listening to all the good and obvious and satisfactory and reasonable transportational inventions the remaining twenty-one or twelve or five students before you have come up with. Until, at last, it's time for you to share your big idea. Which is no longer big. Is, in fact, small and weak and cowering. An idea that will serve to impress no one. Change nothing.

Beaten, bereft, disheartened, you mumble, "A super no-gas truck?" and your life goes on. And on.

But what you may not realize is that there was something to be learned on that day. A life lesson, as it were. A truth. To wit: Being first with a great idea is hard. Being last with a great idea is even harder.

15} Evil in Tent

I love road trips. Always have. But before setting out on America's blue highways, before I make my first wrong turn or erupt in my first episode of road rage, I have to decide: Camping or hotels? The choice, of course, is critical. It will determine my budget, what clothes to pack, the sightseeing hours I'll lose to SpectraVision porno, the proportion of my diet that is "musical fruit," and whether a series of grisly bellboy murders will stymie several local police forces. This time out, clearly foreseeing the requisite, complimentary copy of *USA Today* that I would find outside my hotel room door on a daily basis, I opt for camping.

Little known fact: most state and national park campgrounds are segregated. That is, tent (or so-called "primitive") campers (like me) and RV/trailer campers (Republicans) have their own completely separate areas. And, "Ya-hoo!" to that. Believe me, I've pitched my tent in "integrated" campgrounds before, and I find it somewhat disconcerting and more than a little discouraging to be noshing trail mix by bug-flittering lantern-light as my neighbors, co-captains of a campground QEII, kick back in their massage recliners, bake lasagna in the Viking, and loudly guess the killer on an eight-year old *Diagnosis Murder* that's blaring away on the thirty-two-inch Sony via satellite dish as they wait for the concierge to arrange front row seats for that evening's Ranger Rudy's Nature Program at the park amphitheater.

By the time I roll into the tent campground, my choice of site is decidedly limited. I wind up wedged between, on one side, a graying biker couple with a shared passion for sleeveless denim garments, clogged pores, and fistfuls of Pizzeria Combos, and, on the other, a crew of male twenty-somethings whose unrestrained beer guzzling fuels such relentless torrents of open-air urination that I fully expect the fire danger level will be downgraded from very high to moderate by morning.

There's a huge difference between pitching the tent I own now and pitching the first one I ever owned. Used to be, I'd have to prop up, stake out, line rig, circle-inspect-adjust, circle-inspect-tweak, *ad nauseum,* performing a ritual dance of perplexed machismo and fear of wind. Now, thanks to intelligent-design fiberglass connecting rods, NASA-developed four-season synthetic textiles plus state-of-the-art architectural engineering by MIT's Environmental Structures Lab, I have a tornado/blizzard-proof tent that goes up in two minutes flat. (I confess I still haven't figured out exactly how to set up the damn thing's basement.) The downside of such a sophisticated tent (besides, of course, its thirty-year mortgage) is that it's clearly embarrassed to be seen with me.

I whip up dinner on my miniature propane camp stove. Amazingly, it's able to miniaturize the taste of anything cooked on it.

Damn. After dinner I feel the need to use the bathroom. And in this particular park, that means (gasp!) a pit toilet. I tell myself I will *not* join my neighbors *en flagrante eliminato,* even if it means sitting on a piss-spattered seat above a dank underground caldron of invidious Ebola virus, fetidly percolating in ninety-eight-degree August heat. However, my own internal turn of phrase proves too vivid and I'm moved to drive the forty-mile roundtrip to the McDonald's in town for relief.

As the moon climbs higher in the night sky, I stop adding wood to my campfire. The flames die, leaving a bed of vermilion embers. Time to turn in. The trick, I find, to getting a good night's sleep while camping is knowing what to expect. And I do. So when the perfect, level, leaf-cushioned plot where I've pitched my tent turns out to be a thin-sodded grid of spine-seeking, spine-jabbing roots and rocks that can be felt through tent floor, foam cushion, down sleeping bag, and the axon-extinguishing effects of a spleef the size of Shaquille O'Neal's thumb, I'm fully prepared: I move to the car. When a mosquito inevitably starts singing its song deep, deep, deep in the pit of my ear, no problem: I spray my ears full of Raid Yard Guard. And when the dead-of-night grumblings, rustlings, and crunchings of wild critters wake me, I suffer no rush of city-boy anxiety. I know just what to do: I lean forward and politely ask the biker couple to please get out of my front seat and go finish their Combos at their own campsite.

Breaking camp is always a wetter task than I remember, morning dew on everything. I shake the shakeable, wipe the wipeable, sponge the spongeable, squeegee the squeegeeable, sun dry the wipes, sponge, and squeegee. By 2 P.M., I'm on the road. Projecting to my next stop. A stop bound to test my ability to survive an uncivilized, untended, inhospitable environment: the nearest Motel 6.

16 } Working Out (Some Issues)

Bitter winds sweep south into the U.S. from the frigid nation that pioneered the flannel-lined cocktail dress; thermometers in the Northeast, Mideast, and Midwest show less mercury than Charlie the Tuna's last blood test; unrelenting steel gray clouds have extinguished the sun as completely as Tom DeLay has extinguished his own humanity; snow so plagues and oppresses us that men, instead of urinating their names into its white dominion, now urinate suicide notes. Clearly, friends, wintertime is no time to exercise outdoors. Wintertime is joining-a-gym-time.

My first step is turning on the TV. I figure with all the fitness club commercials airing at this time of year, I'll be able to review what's available without wasting a lot of energy running around town. And I'm right. In a single evening, I see ads for a trio of big-spending rivals, all anxious to differentiate themselves in a highly competitive market sector. One facility implies that my every workout will be done next to an affable, buxom, hot (but-not-in-a-sweaty-way) babe; another suggests my every workout will be done among *several* affable, buxom, hot (but-not-in-a-sweaty-way) babes; the last seems to indicate that their clientele will regard *me* as an affable buxom, hot (but-not-in-a-sweaty-way) babe. After much mulling, I go with the "several babes" option.

* * *

My initial visit to the gym exceeds my wildest expectations. I drop six pounds in a grueling, marathon session of sweat, strain and pain. When I finally crack and sign the five-year contract, however, the salesperson eases up, tosses me a towel, unlocks his office door and points me toward the locker room.

Ah, the locker room. Where men whom I would classify as overexposed if they were hatless wander about buck-naked. Where skin conditions, scars, protuberances, medical oddities, lapses of hygiene and ravages of time, gravity and Entenmanns's that should unquestionably remain hidden from anyone save the coroner, are exposed with abandon. This is a room mad with *sculptures* of Dorian Gray. Conversely, there are several Adonises (Adoni?) creating their own tableau of raw swagger and six-packs. I find these serious, sculpted, rippling, flexing, v-shaped guys to be more than a little intimidating. This may be due to the fact that I see one of them remove a ten-pound dumbbell from his locker and curl it with his penis.

I have never felt comfortable being naked in a crowd. I am woefully self-conscious of everything from my stark whiteness (I reflect so much light I do not cast a shadow) to my physique (imagine the adult offspring of a bag of onions and a lightbulb). As a result, when in a locker room situation, the time that elapses between my street clothes being off and my exercise togs being on can be measured in picoseconds. A remarkable feat when one considers I carry out this task inside a closed locker.

The facilities are truly sumptuous. There's an Olympic-sized swimming pool (actually, after careful measurement, I discover it's only Goodwill Games-sized). Aerobics classes (including the latest: Absolut Low Impact, a workout which involves languidly swaying to music while sipping Screwdrivers from a sports bottle). Aisle after aisle of treadmills, stationary bikes, recumbent bikes, stair climbers, ski simulators, rowing machines, elliptical rocking chairs, hand-cranked ice cream machines, Curly Joe Howard PowerWheels (large turntables that people lay down on then run in circles using a shoulder as a pivot point), even programmable Whack-a-Moles with weighted whackers and built-in heart-rate monitors. A favorite area seems to be the Exercise Yard, where people with fewer than ten years-to-life on their hands can simulate the anaerobic/resistance workout of America's finest physical specimens: our hardened—and hard-bodied—cons.

Another unexpected feature of this health club is the ubiquity of TV. There are banks and banks of televisions that can be (and *are* being) watched (and listened to, via headphones) everywhere. Whether one chooses to run or bike, swim or sauna, play racquetball or do yoga. And while I appreciate the effort being made to keep me mindlessly entertained while I exercise, it turns out I really don't enjoy gazing at the cool perfection of celebrities while straining along with a roomful of smelly, drippy, jiggling three-dimensional shlubs. It makes me feel as if we're doing the all work but they're reaping all the benefits.

Not being a "people person" (according to the quiz I took in a recent *Esquire,* I'm a "cartoon character person"), my greatest adjustment is in "sharing" my workout space and time. I'm used to running alone, biking alone, tug-of-war-ring alone. No more. Not here. Now I'm a towel-carrying citizen of Spandex Nation. Laboring cheek-to-jowl with people who I can tell are silently condemning my cheeks and my jowls. Breathing deep into my lungs the atomized secretions and evaporating emissions of fetid strangers. But mostly feeling burned, as the affable, buxom, hot (but-not-in-a-sweaty-way) babes I'm surrounded by are a pregnant woman and her lesbian lover, a colossus who tells me this is her last stop before stomach stapling surgery and a grandmother wearing a T-shirt that declares, "Estrogen is for pussies."

Not surprisingly, I have decided I will not be returning to the gym. I do not belong. I cannot adapt. I will not get past my urge to coldcock the guy with the sharp creases in his gym shorts. Instead, I will suck it up and take my exercise in the cold and the gray and the wind and the snow. As for my training table, I suppose I'll be eating my five-year contract.

17 } I See Dead People. Most of Them Me.

It's a beautiful, sun-saturated pre-noon, and I'm hugging the faded center stripe on a stretch of rural two-lane. I've resisted putting the top down on my Miata because there's nothing more clichéd than an open-cockpitted convertible gliding under a glorious blue ceiling. And I don't do clichés. Unless you count the way I use the word "do."

Smack in front of me is a pick-up truck. A high-rider with tires of such fearful proportions I imagine they're the tires regular tires pray to. The vehicle's black exterior is succumbing to a blotchy rash of primer edged with an incurable, creeping cancer of rust. We both clip along at about sixty-five mph and it occurs to me that maybe I'm following a little too closely because I find I'm able to check my teeth in the reflection off the polished chrome ball of the truck's trailer hitch. After I determine they're all there, I ease off a couple car lengths. One regular, one Matchbox.

This backed-off angle shows me a kid sitting in the truck bed near the tailgate pinching bundles of slender fries from a grease-spotted fast-food bag. I guess him at about ten, though his "I solved Stonehenge" T-shirt makes him seem older. He's riding next to a dog, a big old mean, sinewy coonhound that looks like a repository of vicious behavior and, I suspect, hunts the omnivorous nocturnal mammal of his nomenclature with a handgun. The glare he drops over the tailgate at me suggests fugitives are a significant part of his pedigree. And that anthropomorphism is a significant part of mine.

Curves, hills, and the occasional oncoming car won't let me get past the pick-up. Which is really too bad and suddenly worse as the truck hits a bump, a sharp welt in the blacktop, and bucks, I can't help hyper-descriptively noting, in much the same way a snake-bit rodeo bronc having a methamphetamine seizure would. Boy and dog are tossed high, made airborne. They seem to hang briefly as their ride speeds out from under them. But they don't hang. Not for a second. So there's no time to react. To their descent. As a unit. Into my windshield. Through it. And in a percussive chaos of affordable Japanese engineering, youth, golden shoestring potatoes, dog breath, and thirty-two recently inventoried teeth, I'm fatally killed dead. Crushed and extinguished like a cigarette butt in an ancient Smoky the Bear PSA.

No. Wait. That's not right. The rise in the roadway was only *potentially* that violent. The boy/beast/potato death-medley never left the truck bed. I'm unscathed. Safe (to be shot by spree killers in the convenience store up the road). In one piece (for the trachea-obstructing trout bone that will dispatch me at dinner). Wholly whole (only to be snuffed in my sleep tonight by the creeping malignance of carbon monoxide leaking from my furnace).

But for now I'll just drive. And try to make the horizon by nightfall.

18 } SOP FAQs

I am a busy man. My time is tight, my schedule full, my patience short. To streamline my social interaction and thus save precious minutes and seconds, below you will find my *permanent* answers to life's most common questions. If, in the future, you should find yourself in my company, please note that I will no longer entertain in-person, oral iterations of these questions, but will instead proceed directly to the substance of our discussion or the business we have to transact. Should you require further instruction on how to use this form, don't ask.

Pleasantries

How are you?
I'm fine as the pinfeather fluff around a chicken's anus.

What's new?
In terms of the cosmos, earth. In terms of the earth, life. In terms of life on earth, humans. In terms of humanity, me. In terms of me, one too many Carl Sagan books.

What's up?/Wassup?
By court order, my fly.

What's shakin'?
All items heretofore designated for bakin'.

What've you been up to lately?
My days are split evenly between trying to broker a land-for-peace deal between Jerry and Dick Van Dyke, obtaining clinical proof that intestinal fortitude is not a substitute for dietary fiber, traveling to a merry dream world where my annual prostate exam takes the form of a written test and rechoreographing the Bunny Hop for the wheelchair-bound.

How about this weather?
Terrible. It gives any simpleton license to make conversation.

Relationships

Do I make you happy?
That depends. How many more questions are there?

What happened to the kind, caring man I fell in love with?
I kicked his ass outta here after he made a pass at me.

What do you think you're doing?
At this moment, I believe my actions could be described as "pre-prosecuted."

Do you know how that makes me feel?
Instead of guessing whether "Yes" or "No" is the least wrong response to your question, I will simply move my head in small ambiguous circles.

How could you?
A grievous combination of Viagra and Barry White music.

Will you please leave me alone?
I'd be happy to. Keep in mind, however, that with over six billion people on the planet, even if I work 24/7/365, it will take me several years to eliminate every last one of them.

Was it good for you?
I think so. But then anything that elevates one's heart rate, works multiple muscle groups, and burns calories is "good for you," isn't it?

Out and About

Do you know why I pulled you over?
Absolutely. You've randomly selected me from the thousands of traffic violators sharing this highway in order that I may be the next victim of your ongoing ego-feeding power trip, *or* you're a delusional control freak with an unrealistic view of your role in bringing order to an inherently disorderly world, probably the result of a chaotic or abusive childhood, *or* you want to enforce your parochial, nay, fascistic interpretation of the traffic code by forcing me to give up my monkey chauffeur.

Can I help you find something?
Yes. Please locate with your hands my vas deferens.

How would you like to pay for that?
I would like to calculate the square root of the total price and give you that amount in Canadian dollars.

Who's next?
On what Who album will you find "Won't Get Fooled Again?" 1970s Hit Singles for $1,000, Alex.

Paper or plastic?
I'm 100 percent plastic.

Do you have any coupons?
No. Before I left the house, I decided to try to get through a whole day without looking like a loser.

May I take your order?
Yes. Klaatu. Barada. Nikto.

Got any change?
Yes. Except I prefer to call it my tech stock portfolio.

Hey, shithead, are you lookin' *to get your ass kicked?*
No. But through sheer dumb luck it would appear I've stumbled on the perfect opportunity.

Personal
Have you been drinking?
Have you been breathing?

Don't you ever get tired of sitting on your ass?
Yes. And when that happens, I go to bed.

Could you hurry up?
Sorry, no. Hurrying is for Jack Russell Terriers, the hyperactive, meth freaks, silent movie comedians, and people who have always wanted to meet Pope John Paul II.

What's wrong *with you?*
Gastroesophageal reflux disease, sinusitis, swine flu, dropsy,

mopishness, hammer toes (three), low cheekbones, lazy eye, bashful bladder, arrogant sternum, stationary carsickness, seasonal impotence, willful incontinence, neat-freakishness, flimflam on the flippity-flop, flaunting-o mi perfecto Spanglish todo el time-o, spandex frenzy, and chronic listing syndrome (both types, the inner ear disorder that causes one to stand several degrees off perpendicular and the neurotic tendency to itemize).

Are you nuts or something?
If you define "nuts" as "continuing to do the same thing but expecting different results," then yes. If, however, you define "nuts" as "continuing to do the same thing but expecting different results," then yes again.

Why can't you ever finish anything you start?
Damned if I.

19 } Somewhere Between Red and Orange

I was having breakfast when the authorities burst into my apartment. "Robert W—," the official in charge said, "you will please to come with us." His manner was so utterly threatening, it's possible I only imagined the Teutonic affectation in his sentence construction.

"May I at least finish my cereal?" I inquired, indicating the bowl full of sweet, fruit-flavored spheres I'd just poured milk over.

"Silly, Robert. Trix are for fat kids with sugar-induced hypertension," he said, putting a savagely frank twist on the beloved brand's theme line. "Take him away."

Two men in dark suits flanked me, each gripping one of my arms. As I gauged the breadth of their shoulders, the size of their arms, their overall bulk and brawn, I was certain of just one thing: they hadn't bought off-the-rack.

The suits moved me roughly through the foyer, out the front door and out onto the porch. "But what do you want with me?" I asked. "What have I done?" The sun was barely up and the painted wood of the porch stairs was cool on my bare feet, as if I were wearing archless, topless shoes made of painted porch wood.

"What do you *think* you have done?" he responded.

"I can't imagine," I said, all the while wondering if the plans I had for the upcoming evening might be construed, in the strictest legal sense, as "conspiracy to commit drunk and disorderly," and, if they could, when I would have found the time to inform on myself. "I lead a very ordinary life."

"Yes, perhaps," he said, as I was forced into the back seat of a black sedan and bound tightly, inescapably, to the seat by a strap that not only diagonally crossed my torso but traversed my lap then clicked tightly into a steel buckle. "But you would do well to remember that you are dealing with people who are very well informed."

We spent the next two hours driving in circles, trying to find a way out of my housing development.

Inevitably, we arrived at headquarters. There, a uniformed guard led me to a small, windowless chamber with a high ceiling and plain white walls. A single, bare lightbulb hung in the center of the room. The bulb was overbright for the stark, confined space; I wondered how many suspects had been forced to sign confessions here and how they could possibly have been expected to read them over beforehand with so much harsh, reflective glare. Spread beneath the fixture was a plastic sheet covered in large, multicolored polka-dots; I recognized it as the "game board" from the game of Twister. I recoiled at the inhuman and humiliating possibilities.

As if reading my thoughts, the guard said, "The hardwood floors have just been refinished and we're using that to keep the scratches to a minimum till the rug we ordered is delivered," whereupon he brought a hard, straight-backed chair into the room, set it on the plastic, left and locked the door. I sat. Alone. With little choice but to consider precisely how much a few potted plants might soften the room's look.

I'd been sitting, waiting for nearly an hour when the door

opened. A bespectacled, middle-aged gentleman in a drab suit entered. My anxiety rising, my mind racing, I wondered if interrogations at Scotland Yard were conducted by inspectors in drab kilts and what a drab kilt would look like, exactly.

The man was followed into the room by a woman in her thirties carrying a note pad and pencil, obviously his subordinate. Their faces were in stark contrast: his grim, hers smiling. Or so I thought. After a moment, I realized the bun in the woman's hair was pulled and twisted so tightly at her crown that it drew the corners of her mouth up and back.

The guard reentered with two more chairs, beanbags this time, plainly determined to protect the room's pristine floor. He placed the limp, voluminous, vinyl furnishings opposite mine and left, closing the door behind him.

The man and woman lowered themselves deliberately into their chairs. Before long, he cleared his throat and began to speak, whereupon she immediately started taking notes. *This is all some sort of bizarre nightmare,* I thought. *Who would hire a full-time stenographer when a twenty-dollar tape recorder could do the same job?*

The man introduced himself as Inspector P—. "I have several questions to put to you," he said. "When you have answered them to my satisfaction, you will be free to go. Answer them in less than sixty seconds and I'll fly you and a companion to Las Vegas where you'll stay at the fabulous Caesars Palace where guests are entertained nightly by singer extraordinaire, Celine D—."

You have nothing to hide, I told myself. *Cooperate fully.* Yet nagging, gnawing at my very essence was the reality that in all encounters with the authorities, caution is one's sole protection. Only grief, misfortune, and misery could possibly come from any collaboration. I'd learned that lesson only too well when I was a junior in high school and, at my father's urging, had adopted the Maytag Repairman "look."

"W— is an Arab name, isn't it?" Inspector P— asked.

"Um, Swiss, in fact," I informed him, neutrally. My interrogator removed his eyewear, then folded and slipped them into the soft leatherette case protruding from his shirt pocket. He looked younger without his glasses, a compliment I decided to withhold until I might really need it. After a moment, he took some documents from an inside jacket pocket and shuffled through them methodically, unhurriedly. I tried to read the reflected pages in his pupils but found the text too small, too backward, and, when I really thought about it, none of my beeswax.

Suddenly, he lifted his eyes from the papers and fixed them on me. His gaze was heinous: icy, punishing, cutting, withering. I prayed he would not turn it on my penis.

"Can you account for your whereabouts on February 2—, 200—?"

"Um, well, uh, let's see, I, uh, that, er . . ." I stammered, as if teaching a graduate course in stammering. "February 2—, 200—, you say?"

"No. I said, 'February 2—, 200—,'" he corrected.

"Oh, so sorry," I replied, all courtesy and ass-kiss. "In that case no, I'm afraid I can't account for my whereabouts. But only because that's a week from next Thursday."

The Inspector accepted my answer without reaction. He again looked through his documents: reading, shuffling, reading. His tongue slid slowly between his lips, as if to say, "Could anyone else eat a Slim Jim right now?" Without looking at him directly, I watched him tug on his left earlobe, spin (twice) the gold wedding band on his ring finger, then wind his watch. The artful bastard. My chance to see Celine D— was ticking away with his blasted tics.

At this point, Inspector P— struggled out of his beanbag and, gaining his feet, circled around me, coming to a stop directly behind my chair. I didn't dare turn around. Abruptly, he launched a belligerent barrage of rapid-fire inquiries, making me feel both assaulted and a-peppered.

"You own an Afghan hound. Does he have ties to terrorists?"

"No, he's destroyed all my shoes and carpeting without any organized support network."

"Do you favor the views of Ayatollah Khomeini or Ayatollah Sistani?"

"The one who never smiles and has the beard."

"Have you had any associations with the Axis of Evil within the past year?"

"Absolutely not. I would never go to a Yankees' game *or* a Walmart store."

"What celebrity looks most like Yasser Arafat?"

"Ringo Starr."

"Do you want to spin or solve?"

"I'll have to spin, Inspector. Come o-o-on, big money . . ."

Then, silence. Complete and utter silence. Except for the pencil scratches of the stenographer as she noted the complete and utter silence. Minutes passed. Time dragged. Soon, I found myself imagining a pocket watch immersed in a jar of molasses buried deep in permafrost, something I rarely do when I'm not talking on the phone with my Mom.

Finally, The Inspector spoke again. "You're free to go now," he informed me, dismissively. With that, he walked over to his subordinate, helped extricate her from the beanbag chair, and both strode smartly across the room and out the door, which they did not close. I was left alone. Apparently free. And whether I'd been illegally detained in the first place or released in error, the important thing right now was that the system worked.

My relief was deep. Staggering. Yet a lingering sense of desolation remained. And that, I knew, was there to stay. But a bowl of milk-swollen, wasted Trix waiting at home will do that to a person.

20 } I Feel My Pain

I wake to pain. Brute, serious, pure pain. In my head. No. *Of* my head. Like my brain's been out working a second job as a soccer ball. No, really. Something's wrong. Very wrong. Wrong to the point where I'd consider a guillotine the cautious approach to correcting it.

An inventory: The muscles of my jaw throb with the insistence of a romance novel's hero's manhood. My lips cramp. Thick, aching, and miserable, my tongue lies languid in my maw, dead as the debate over fluoridation. Worst of all, though, is the implacable pressure of twenty pounds of unnamed shame and vague remorse stuffed into my five-pound skull. I need aspirin. Aspirin stuffed with Percocet and chemically coated in a hard OxyContin shell.

Jeez-us! What the hell happened? What exactly did I do last night to deserve the heartless head I have this morning? Think, person with the name that's not accessible right now but who's operating this brain, think...

Okay. Let's see. There was the party. Rolled in there about 9:30, 10:00. Crowd moderate, music cranked. Checked my cape and deerstalker...bummed and smoked a clove cigarette ...scarfed some Chex Mix...a Rice Krispie Treat...a couple of Froot Loops in a Blanket...blew out my wrist ligaments playing Ultimate Cribbage ... bummed and smoked a ham-and-clove cigarette...took part in a tableau vivant of Ensor's *Christ's Entry into Brussels in 1889*...limbo'd under the Irish Wolfhound

…there was conversat…Oh, God! No! That's right. Fuh-and-uck. There was *conversation*.

No. Excuse me. That's not entirely accurate. Better I should say there was talking. Yowzah, was there talking. Copious, bounteous, plenteous talking. A torrent of talking. With still more talking to bridge the occasional silences when there was no talking. And, assholeassholeasshole that I am, damn near all of this chin music poured from *my* mouth. Damn near all of it about *me*. No doubt this is why I now have a head that feels like it's been stuffed with steel wool, formaldehyde, and Stratocaster feedback. Because last night, foolishly, recklessly, narcissistically, and regretfully, I seriously and completely over-self-indulged myself. Again.

Which was definitely not the plan. But then, in my experience, becoming intoxicated by—or at least insensate to—the sound of one's own voice is *never* the plan. It just happens. Unconsciously. Against your own better judgement. Like a trip to Orlando. Or sitting through a whole episode of *Everybody Loves Raymond*. As a recovering monologaholic once said to me, it starts subtly, ends uglily. Or something.

So, but, where did I go wrong last night? Well, um, let me rewind a ways here…

I remember going into the party with a truly generous frame of mind, absolutely hell-bent to ask questions. To be curious and an active listener. And early on, I was. I delved. Volleyed. Gave more than took. Happily accepting the role of lubricant in the evening's social intercourse, i.e.:

"You're a patent attorney from Milwaukee? Wow. Talk at length about patent law. Then do the same about Milwaukee," I solicited. "What did Rush Limbaugh tell his *next* caller?" I asked. "Does all paté give you the runs or just certain kinds?"

I probed. "You can recite the long version of *Alice's Restaurant* verbatim? You'll have to prove that," I encouraged.

That didn't last long, though. An hour maybe, sixty-one minutes tops. Making it probably a little before 11 when I started slipping. Weakened, excited, tempted, I think, by all the first- person pronouns being enjoyed by those around me. (Christ! What rationalization! A flashing neon sign of self-centered denial.)

I started prudently enough. Just a little taste of agreement ("I'm against gun control, too, but I'd still like you to quit pointing that thing at me."). Next I tossed off a couple of shrewd observations. ("I never see movies the first week they're out. I like the actors to get comfortable in their roles.") Then— *wham!*—just like that, I was gone, spewing the hard stuff: strong opinion ("I mean, come on, there must be a dozen reasons Ellie May would've been better off marrying Dash Riprock than Sonny Drysdale. First, he wasn't a mama's boy. Second ..."), overly detailed, wildly tangential personal narratives ("The fourth time I went to the guy, he says the cankers should be gone by now and he's not sure why they're not, which is exactly what my boss says about his kids, who are both living at home even though they've graduated from college, one from Michigan State, I think, no, Michigan U., talk about a party school ...) and life philosophies ("Believe me, originality is just a tired idea in front of the right people ...")

By 12:30, I was pretty sloppy. I remember my speech getting all slurry as my mouth muscles got tired, sore. Yet, for the life of me, I couldn't stop. Or be stopped. (Like the old saying goes, "One discursion is too many and a thousand aren't enough.") I yielded the floor rarely and reluctantly. To me, the responses, input, and conversational contributions of others were as superfluous as restraint at a *Jerry Springer* taping.

Oooh. Wait. A particularly appalling display is just bubbling up. A not-quite-dim-enough memory of being introduced to a woman who, the introducer just manages to get in edgewise as I'm straining to swallow a sticky, silencing s'more, worked at the U.S. Embassy in South Africa and who, at a formal reception there, actually got to meet and speak with Nelson Mandela. Well, the woman didn't get to spit out more than a "Hello" before I launched into a twenty-minute riff on the Ladysmith Black Mambazo concert I went to where some guy at the concession stand had given me back change for $10 instead of the $20 I'd given him. Then, somehow, because I couldn't really do Nelson Mandela, I segued into a few minutes of my Desmond Tutu impression.

And what's so weird about this kind of rude behavior is that not once the whole night did it register with me that I'd become a serial monologist. That I was not so much holding court as holding captives. How is it that at no point did I think, *Why isn't anyone else's mouth moving?* But I guess that's the book on habitual over-self-indulgence: It's all about me, it's none about you. Except for the part where you listen.

Anyway, the last thing I remember was at some point—this must have been very late—reenacting my triumph as "Mr. Ketchup" in my 3rd grade class's Condiment Pageant. About half way through that, things go blank. I guess I blacked out. Apparently, even I couldn't take any more me.

As for what happened next, what time I left the party, how I got home, into bed, stuff like that, I don't know. I was totally out. Oblivious. Until now. Until this cranium of painium. Which, to be honest, is abating. Must be all this retelling of events. Events involving *me*. Hair of the dog, you know?

21 } A Series of Mild Strokes

8:45 A.M. [Greenback Harbor Country Club]: I am not a golfer. Which is exactly why Clay, Trey, and Dave asked me to shoot a round with them this morning. Today I will be playing the role of the buffoon. The schmuck. And considering the raves I've received over the years for my portrayals of "My Son, the Knucklehead," "Teen Goofball," "Jobless Twit," and "Bob, The Bungling Lover," I feel quite confident I can bring this part to life, too.

9:00 [1st tee]: The morning air is bracing, stimulating. I feel alive, vigorous, unleashed. I top my Titleist 6 badly off the tee, and it dribbles forward about eight yards, whereupon we all pile into the golf cart and drive out to the ball for my second shot.

9:13 [2nd hole]: A 406-yard dogleg right with a water hazard. Par is five. I shoot a Par^2.

10:28 [3rd green]: We're all finishing our third Bloody Mary. The rule today is we each have to drink one cocktail per hole. Clay boldly suggests one per stroke would have been more fun. I remind him I'm currently shooting thirty-nine and that that particular rule change would make me dead by now. Clay seems to think my remark is supportive of his.

10:44 [4th tee]: The foursome behind us asks to play through. Just looking at these elitist, exclusionary, leisure-class, good old boy-networked, cigar-sucking swine, I'm reminded of exactly why I, a guest here, find country clubs so thoroughly despicable: Sansabelt slacks. Put in a foul mood by this forced exposure to such a sportswear abomination, I confront the old bastards on the issue of why their club doesn't admit women. "Just what are you afraid of?" I ask. The most bulbously beltless member of the group immediately puts me in my place by explaining that the vast majority of men who join country clubs do so less for the golf than for a private, outdoor venue in which to engage in anal sex and that the presence of women on the course would be both unsettling and inhibiting. Live and learn.

10:57 [5th green]: Tough break. I putt from the frog's hair for a "dodeca-bogie," but, misreading the break of the green, sink the ball in my own shirt pocket.

11:11 [well off the 6th fairway]: Looking for my ball deep in a stand of trees off the fairway, I happen to spot a grazing deer. Careful to stay upwind and in the shadows, I steal silently closer. Finally, so close I can hear the crunchy rumination of tender shoots, I spring and beat the beast to a shuddering death with my five iron. Perhaps I'm more frustrated with this game than I realize.

11:25 [7th green]: Feeling pretty darn loose, I launch into my Tiger Woods impression. This involves nothing so much as insisting that everybody call me "Tiger."

11:39 [8th tee]: At this point, I've lost so many balls that Titleist has flown a company representative out to tell me I've been named their "Man of the Year." Along with the framed proclamation, I'm presented with a dozen of their new "Stealth" balls which, I'm told, save duffers like myself the trouble of losing them out on the course by getting pre-lost in the golf bag.

11:52 [9th hole]:Not surprisingly, after nine holes and nine cocktails, I'm driving erratically, recklessly, drunkenly. Very cool and fun, actually, until some muckety-muck gets a hair up his ass and tells me I shouldn't have the cart in the pro shop in the first place.

12:04 [10th hole]: The ball washers on this course do a nice job but, as usual, are mighty rough on the scrotum.

12:17 [near the 11th green]: Against course regulations, I drive the cart into a bunker, where I get stuck. Our efforts to extricate the damn thing cause it to roll onto its side; another push and we get it to roll over, out of the trap, and back onto its wheels. In the process, however, our cooler of Bloody Marys tips and spills; a spicy red puddle spreads over and soaks into the sand. For this bit of bad fortune, I accept the entire blame. Or at least after I've been buried in the bunker, I come around to that view.

12:31 [12th hole]: We get quite excited when we think we've spotted Fred Couples and Phil Mickelson just ahead of us on the course. The excitement fades as we quickly realize none of us has any idea what Fred Couples and Phil Mickelson look like.

12:43: I'm surprised to learn that just as buildings have no 13th floor, golf has no 13th hole.

12:44 [14th hole]: For the first and only time today, I really connect with the ball, driving it two hundred plus yards straight down the fairway on this short Par 3. It skips onto the green and rolls within eighteen inches of the pin. My luck continues as I follow that feat with my best putting of the day, walking away with a cool nine. I consider celebrating by brandishing my putter à la Chi Chi Rodriguez's "swordplay" but decide it's a bit trite. Instead, I wield my club as an "umbrella," make the green my "street," use the "flag" as my streetlamp, and perform Gene Kelly's "Singin' in the Rain" in its entirety. This has the unexpected benefit of the guys insisting I drive from the ladies' tees for the rest of the round.

12:56 [15th fairway]: I return to form and launch a terrible five-iron shot (my third of the hole) down a steep embankment into some tall weeds. After a long search I locate it behind a sizeable rock. When no one is looking, I kick the ball into the clear, saying nothing. I do not take a penalty stroke and play on. For the rest of the hole, I feel quite troubled by my actions. By the time I've holed out, I'm suffering tremendous remorse for my shameful act. Overcome, I fall to my knees, club in hand, and silently pray for forgiveness. Before I can get to "Amen," however, I'm set upon by golfers from all over the course, all running toward me shouting, "Dorf! Dorf! Can I have your autograph?"

1:09 [16th hole]: Seized by a sudden urge to "be one of the guys," I rashly agree to play this hole in the "skins" format.

It's not until I've lost that I'm informed my "skin" will be collected at a postmatch *briss* in the parking lot.

1:21 [17th tee]: Waiting for another foursome to play out the hole, I ask the guys, "Did you ever notice that golf is the only sport on television where most of the commercials are for the equipment—balls, clubs, shoes, clothes—used in the sport?" I pause a beat for my premise to sink in. "I mean, millions of people play baseball in this country but have you ever seen a commercial for a catcher's mask or a fungo bat or those calf-length pants during a televised game? By golf's example, shouldn't there be ads for prosthetic dentistry during hockey games or hair gel during men's figure skating coverage. I'm just waiting for the day I hear, 'Today's sumo wrestling match is brought to you by the good folks at Fujiama Brand® Giant Diapers for Giant Fighting Men.'" I pause again, wait for the laughs. None come. Instead Trey informs me, "Observational humor died about six years ago, dunce."

1:36 [18th green]: Our lack of cocktails—and the creeping clarity of mind that has come with it—is taking a toll. We all now agree that golf is pointless, boring, and idiotic. That its cost in time and money is too dear. After holing out, we decide we'll never play another round of this excruciating game, then climb into the cart for what promises to be our last trip to the clubhouse. Along the way, we review how much money each of us is carrying and, based on the combined tally, decide we have more than enough to repair to the Nineteenth Hole bar and rediscover our love of the game.

22 } Talk the Walk

We are walking against a disease. Or a condition. Or an injustice. Or a deplorable state of affairs. Something. But we are walking. Walking. Miles. Hours. All for money. Promised money. Pledges we've touched our friends and families and neighbors and co-workers for. A dime, quarter, fifty cents, a dollar a mile. Basically the same touches we'd made for last week's Hike to Fight A Lamentable Hardship. And the week before's March Against Some Devastating Misfortune. And that we'll tap again before next Sunday's Walkathon to End Life's Tragic Misery. Uh, Miserable Tragedy.

The turnout is impressive. Apparently, the affliction *du jour* (I've done some asking around and apparently it is an affliction that's our *raison d'être*) is quite popular in a that's-too-bad sort of way. A woman walking next to me says, "This is a lot more people than Making Strides for Blindness had last month." I'd seen a snippet of coverage on the news and knew she was right. "Pfft," I say, trying to be supportive. "Those people who support the blind are such losers."

Our event's lead walker is a television newsreader. Her flawlessly applied Outdoor Morning Light makeup just screams, "I'm an average person ready to walk twenty kilometers early on a Sunday." Her special off-air/active woman coif is not only sufficiently down-to-earth but aerodynamically efficient. Her shoes—Nike Air Compassions, the shoe specifically designed to make short work of any charity walk, getting it out of the way before it screws up the whole goddamn weekend—appear to be either brand-new or just back from the detailers. All fairly typical, really. Organizers ask local celebrities to these events to assure coverage by at least one network affiliate in town, ergo, her pre-20K Mary Kay, et al, is necessary in order for her to face the cameras. None of which explains why she's being attended by a sommelier.

I started walkathoning in 1997. My motivation was and is very powerful, very personal: meeting women. It works, too. I earn sensitivity points just for showing up. (More than one "prospect" has told me sensitivity is an aphrodisiac, which has saved me a fortune on rhino horn.) And I'm assumed to be, at worst, earnest and committed, at best, vigorous and dynamic. (Like you, guys, I'm none of those things.) Plus, many walking women are not only available but are in an especially vulnerable state (read: their bullshit detector is offline), having just lost a significant other or whatever to the cause at hand. It also pays to have a story prepared, one about how the affliction has touched one's life. (Often I take my dog and choke out something all-purpose like, "Without Queenie, I don't think I could cope ...") A tip for novices: Always work the front of the pack. The only women you'll find at the rear are the old, the doughy, and moms pushing strollers.

At the start point, we'd been a milling, eager, concentrated knot of humanity. An hour-and-a-half into the ordeal, we're stretched—cluster-gap-cluster-gap-cluster-gap—over several miles of sidewalk. Esprit wanes. One desperate soul whips out a cell phone and calls the Center for Disease Control, checking to see if the thing we're walking against has by some chance, in the past ninety minutes, been cured, allowing the lot of us to bail without shame. There's no answer. Speculation that if there's no one at the CDC *everything must be cured* dies less quickly than one would imagine. This is also when you begin to hear the word "Bataan" turn up in conversations. And the sardonic call, "dead man walkathoning."

For anyone considering doing one of these walks, one item is de rigueur: the fanny pack. Women, I observe, put these to good use carrying cell phone, tissues, cotton balls, lip balm, hand cream, sunscreen, hairbrush, energy bar, blister pads, pre-moistened sanitary wipes, needle and thread, pepper spray, insect repellent, snake bite kit, datebook, pen (and back-up pen), mini-White Pages, mini-Yellow Pages, and any number of wrapped and mysterious feminine hygiene products. For men, as far as I can tell, the fanny pack is worn just in case a thickly accented foreigner rushes up with an anxious plea to hide his Letters of Transit.

At fifteen kilometers, the majority of the group is sweaty and tired, bored and cranky. Caps have been doffed and stuffed in pockets; shirts and sweaters are tied around waists. There's considerably less spring and jiggle in the sundry cellulite-glutted glutes. Some walkers are wondering whatever possessed them to undertake such a foolhardy effort. Phrases like "I don't think I can make it" and "When you think about it, this affliction we're trying to stamp out may exist as an essential part of God's great plan" keep cropping up. Veterans such as myself, however, do not succumb to such defeatist meditations; we suck it up, stay focused, then fall in behind a particularly wide-bodied strider and draft.

Any number of injuries can befall such a large group on such a lengthy hike. Muscle strains, ankle sprains, knee twists, leg and foot cramps, scratches and scrapes, bug bites and stings, sunburn, allergic reactions, shortness of breath, and dehydration are the most common. On occasion, some asshole who's seriously desperate for attention will suffer a heart attack. Because so much can go wrong, event organizers generally arrange for an ambulance or medical personnel to be standing by somewhere on the route. I find if you ask nicely, they'll gladly give you a reenergizing blast on the bum with the defibrillator. As far as actual injuries go, though, in all the "thons" I've done, I've only suffered one. And without getting into the whole megillah, let me just offer this caveat: If you ever fake a heart attack, do your ribcage a favor and "regain consciousness" before the CPR is administered.

Somewhere around the 18K mark, with the finish line tantalizingly within grasp, a second wind sweeps through our ranks. With it comes the nearly rhetorical question, "What should we do when we're done here?" The leaving-nothing-to-chance answer? "Let's get something to eat." But what, exactly? Will it be pizza? A brunch buffet? Cheeseburger and fries? Ice cream? It hardly matters. The important thing, clearly, is to bury the one-thousand-calorie deficit we've each earned over the past three-plus hours under a three-to-five-thousand-calorie "reward." Without delay. I begin to wonder if the popularity and frequency of these various activity-athons might lie at the ironic root of America's obesity epidemic.

By the time we reach the finish and collect our complimentary "cause" T-shirts, I've linked up with Rita, a lovely young woman. She tells me she's a very active "causewalker," logging miles in the fights against AIDS, genital herpes, syphilis, gonorrhea, venereal warts, and the first ever Steps to Stomp Crabs. I can't quite decide if all that's good or bad news for me.

23 } Negotiable Bondage

It is late. We are on the road. On the outskirts of Gary, Indiana. Returning home to Chicago, non-Indiana. I look into Greta's eyes; they are filled with tears.

At first, I'm certain they are simply the tears shed by all visitors to Gary: tears of disconsolation and airborne industrial particulates. Yet, perplexingly, her weeping grows in intensity even as we gain distance—ten, fifteen, twenty miles—from the city limits. I can't help remembering that the last time Greta cried so profusely a Kennedy had been killed. Or, possibly, had killed someone.

"What is it?" I ask. "What is causing you such despair?"

"My feet are throbbing in agony," she sobs. "I don't think I can walk one more step." Her assessment is unfortunate since the exit for home is still thirteen miles farther down the highway. To comfort her, I lie and tell her it's only twelve. With a weak, clumsy kick at a dingy possum that is either roadkill or desperately dehydrated, she cries, "Please, darling, please, I want us to buy a car."

There is so much passion in her voice. Such longing. She turns her head slightly left and her lachrymose eyes glisten in the interstate's oncoming headlights. I find I am greatly aroused. As well as in total agreement. Because, clearly, if we possessed the car she so desires, we could be having sex in it right now.

* * *

Our lives have not always been carless. For a very brief period in the mid-1980s we owned and drove a (used) Cocktail Wienie-mobile, the more fuel efficient, sub-compact version of the full-size Wienermobile. ("Weinies" were produced from 1979 through 1986 in limited quantities by the Oskar Meyer Motor-werks in Biefpörkundphiller, West Germany). I was quite fond of the car until, one stifling summer day in a rather bleak part of town, it broke down. Having little choice, I set off on foot in search of an auto repair shop and, after walking dozens of sweltering blocks, found one. Once inside the garage, I approached a rather sturdy, stocky mechanic whose conspicuous veneer of grease began at his boot soles and reached a crescendo at his pompadour. With a tone of bright expectation, I inquired if he could, "get my Wienie humming." I woke up two days later in St. Vincent's Hospital, badly contused and with a neurotic hostility toward my car. We sold it soon after my release.

A few years after that, Greta's parents in Madison, Wisconsin, purchased a new Lincoln Town Car for us as a gift. This impressive act of largesse was magnified by the fact that they had it shipped to us via FedEx Overnight. Within hours of its arrival, we determined that an American luxury sedan is far too much car for a childless couple each of whom weigh less than three hundred pounds and who haven't stuffed a kidnapped, bloated industrialist into a trunk since their days at university. We also soon discovered that the car was meant to facilitate and obligate us to more frequent visits to Greta's parents. The very idea that anyone, especially family, would think our time and attention could be bought hurt and psychologically scarred us both. So much so that we sued them (successfully) for several thousand dollars in punitive damages that we used to cover the cost of our therapy and some therapeutic home theater equipment. When we had the car returned (UPS Ground!) to my in-laws, it was filled with the stench of our displeasure, something our family internist could not explain nor our local car wash eradicate.

The long periods we've lived without an automobile have only been possible because we reside in a large city with an excellent public transportation system. For us, commuting to work is as simple and painless as a ten-minute walk (ten-minute ski in winter) to the train station, changing trains twice, a short bus ride, and a brisk fifteen-minute walk (or ski) to our offices. But we also find public transportation appealing in a larger, more collective sense, in that it keeps us in touch with the people, the masses, the great unwashed and un-deodorant-ed. Everyday we see and make nominal eye contact with countless citizens who are far outside our usual circle of acquaintances. People who are not the least bit ashamed to do Find-a-Words in public, who vote for third and fourth party presidential candidates, even some, I feel certain, who believe a free three-day Florida vacation in exchange for attending a one hour seminar about time-share opportunities sounds like a capital idea.

With the purchase of a car, this mingling with the masses will no longer be part of our day. I can't help but feel that we will be far poorer, though less susceptible to ringworm, lice, and other parasites, for it. How *they* will feel about *our* absence is to presume they have feelings.

Greta and I consider the task of finding a safe, reliable, affordable vehicle a most serious responsibility. Subsequently, to obtain as much relevant data as possible, we split into two one-member teams, each with specific assigned areas of investigation.

My quest entails distilling and collating information from myriad sources, including auto industry Web sites and annual reports; automotive trade magazines; consumer watchdog publications; newspaper reviews of new makes and models; the advice and recommendations of friends, family and colleagues; and several auto-oriented radio call-in shows, among them *Click & Clack*, *RPMpathy* and, on the local Spanish language station, *La Vida Grease Monkey*. Greta's undertaking is considerably more freeform, more intuitive: the interpretation of automotive advertising messages through a filter of religious philosophy to determine What Would Jesus Do If He Had to Choose Between 0% Financing and a $3,000 Rebate. Unfortunately, our respective research is so complex, so extensive, so prolonged, that before either of us can finish, the automotive model year changes and we must start again from scratch.

Eventually, inevitably, however, our independent investigations do conclude. We coordinate a symposium at which we will reveal our findings to each other. Where we will compare particulars. And make decisions on what exactly we will be basing any further decisions on.

We face each other across the stainless steel Serengeti that is our combination home office desk, dining table, and default impulsive sex surface. I unfold and boot a titanium laptop, on which I've created a forceful and compelling PowerPoint presentation consisting of sixty-seven slides, lavishly illustrated with charts, graphs, tables, spread sheets, and, naturally, a tangentially pertinent *New Yorker* cartoon. Greta, I can't help noticing, holds a simple, single sheaf of paper.

At her loving insistence, I present my findings first. Through the first half dozen slides, she seems aloof and impassive, which I blame on John Williams's banal, predictable score. (I vow this will be the last presentation he does for me.) But before long, her ennui subsides, she becomes engaged, asking me to pause often in order to discuss and analyze the data on the screen. She particularly likes Ben Kingsley's cameo (as The Lifetime Drivetrain Warranty) in slide thirteen.

By slide thirty-six, several key issues have been decided: we will purchase not lease; purchase new not used; and choose Teutonic engineering over the engineering of less arrogant nations. By slide fifty-nine, we know we will opt for sunroof rather than moon roof; a coupe rather than a coo-PAY; all-weather radials rather than four-season radials; cup holders rather than drink holders; "nicely equipped" rather than "equipped as shown;" a horn that plays "La Cucaracha" rather than a horn that plays "Charge;" and a radio without an AM dial rather than risk accidentally tuning in a talk show and contracting cancer of the soul.

With just a handful of slides remaining, Greta abruptly turns away from the computer screen, locks me in her gaze and says, "What you've shown me here is remarkable, indispensible. But I feel I must tell you that despite your chart substantiating the Prevalence of Vestigial Tails Among Car Salesmen, regardless, even, of the statistical correlation between Buick ownership and adult diaper use, all I truly require in any vehicle we purchase is that it both bring out the color of my eyes and repudiate the middle class."

"Darling…" I begin, then, faltering, at a loss, I stop trying to speak and skip to the final graphic, slide sixty-seven. It reads:

Ultimately, any vehicle included in the final consideration set must:

1. Bring out the color of Greta's eyes.
2. Repudiate the middle class.

We embrace, deeply grateful for our shared ethos. After a moment, she whispers softly in my ear. Her words warm and affirm. Because I, too, feel certain Jesus would go for the rebate. Soon, the Serengeti is a-rumble with the force of erotic tectonics.

We stand amidst a sea of new, gleaming German automobiles. (To amuse Greta, I've gone down one long row of vehicles and cocked all the passenger side windshield wipers out away from the glass, giving them a comical *"Sieg heil"* look.) Next to us is the car we wish to buy. Or at least the car that comes closest to satisfying all of our criteria (its repudiation of the middle class is stunning: not only is it the official fleet vehicle of the ACLU, the trunk comes equipped with a fighting cock carrier and the car won't even start if its sensors detect the driver wearing culottes). Phase 1, the search, is over; Phase 2, it would seem, is at hand.

I take a few steps toward the inescapable, the unavoidable, the unthinkable. Greta, staring and impassive, doesn't move, remains rooted to the asphalt.

"Come, my love," I coax. "This has to be done."

Suddenly, fear flashes in Greta's eyes. Or, perhaps, a plea. Actually, it could be disgust. I'm not altogether sure. I must confess, I don't really "speak" eyes very well. But clearly, she's conveying a negative emotion and it's in reaction to what we're about to do. No, *must* do. I move into Greta's field of vision and softly, somberly remind her, "If we're going to buy a car, darling, we *have* to talk to a salesperson." The twisting of her features tells me my words have reached their mark, have penetrated her mind's displeasure centers. I take her hand and move once more toward the dealer showroom. My Greta reluctantly joins me.

"Fuck," she spits.

Unlike the language of eyes, I understand, read, and speak profanity fluently. "'Fuck' is right," I reply.

And why shouldn't the prospective car customer be permitted a few expletives of apprehension? Isn't a fear of and contempt for car salesmen, along with the opposable thumb, and, when sober, an aversion to monkey sex, what separates man from ape? Isn't it?

Who among us can hear the ugly tales of those dark forces who wish to "earn your business" without a chill running down their line of credit? The tales of ghastly pressure applied in an office cubicle context. Of unscrupulous tactics affixed to unctuous, incongruous smiles. Of compulsory undercoating smeared thick over an illusory bottom line. Each tale infused with the unspoken subtext of curiously kempt hair, too much cologne, and garish jewelry.

Still, if Greta and I are ever to own a car, we know we must come face-to-face with the fearsome salesbeast. We push open the door and enter his den. My sense of raw-meatness increases tenfold.

The showroom's atmosphere is charged with a dizzying contradiction of testosterone and sterility. The testosterone, naturally, is easily traced to the pack of predators stalking the cavernous space. The sterility is more complex, a combination and accumulation of elements: the demoralizing decor double-fault of wood grain Formica furnishings atop indoor/outdoor carpeting; daylight filtered through exterior walls consisting of massive panels of tinted glass; pristine, zero-mileage cars un-feng shui-ly arranged and displayed with tires glossily waxed; a two-sided, three-tiered rack of crisp four-color brochures describing in detail the cars not five feet away; a coin-operated coffee machine predating the invention of Cremora; and us.

A salesman approaches. "Hi, folks," he barks with a practiced purr, "how can we help you today?"

"It would be of immense help if you would not call us 'folks,'" Greta informs him. Though I love this woman for her honesty, her comment really has no place here. Not only because it will die of loneliness in this house of lies but also because, should we reach the negotiating stage with our now aggravated salesman, it will cost us thousands.

But for the moment, the salesman maintains his anacondan cool and, after an exchange of boilerplate pleasantries, he craftily ascertains which car we're interested in.

"Which vehicle you interested in?" he asks.

I, having rarely been subjected to such practiced guile, rashly reveal our choice. Damn. He has seized the upper hand.

"Like to take it for a test drive?" he queries.

Oh, how cunning he is. If we say, "Yes" he'll know we're strongly interested in the car and press his advantage; if we say, "No" we could wind up buying a car we've never driven.

But I'm no longer the fool I was several seconds earlier in this encounter, and I adroitly parry his wily thrust. "I think we'd prefer a test *ride,*" I tell him. "Is there someone available to drive us?"

Greta, who must have weighed the same ride/no-ride pros/cons, takes tremendous delight in my clever answer, her expression shifting from dour to detached.

"Yes, there is someone," the salesman concedes. "But I'm afraid she's wearing culottes today."

It is in the picosecond following the period at the end of his response that I realize this will not be our day. Because in that precise moment, I understand this man cannot possibly be outfoxed by the likes of we faux foxes. I grasp that his short sleeve white shirt is an exquisite deception, a sublime *illusion* of professional impotence and individual inadequacy. And I accept that should he, as the sale progresses, throw in free floor mats, it is only so we do not completely lose our faith in humanity. That or the cost is already built into the destination charges.

"The sound system is exceptionally dynamic," Greta observes, nudging the CD player's volume two digits higher. "I've never heard k.d. lang sound so thoroughly homosexual before."

She (Greta, not k.d.) is behind the wheel of our chosen vehicle, driver for the chauffeurless test drive into which our Machiavellian Rasputin of a salesman deviously manipulated us. So far, we've been out on the road for one hour, fifty-three minutes. This is due in part to the stops we've made along the way—for cigarettes (we're addicts), for chocolate (we're addicts), for espresso (we're addicts), for nasal spray (we're addicts), for champagne (we're only human). But more of our time has been spent getting a sense of the car, learning it. Evaluating and analyzing it. Overall, our impressions are positive. Not only has the engine performed powerfully and well, I have looked under the hood and found it to be magnificently incomprehensible. Greta seems quite taken with the handling, which she describes as "deft as a clever metaphor." She also believes the interior's expansive leg- and headroom provide us with an excellent opportunity to, at some future date, append our legs and heads.

"This car is perfect for us," Greta says.

"It is," I respond, smiling.

"It's too much money," she says.

"It is," I respond, smiling.

"But it's possible we'll be able to negotiate a far more equitable price," she says.

"It is," I respond, smiling.

"That's the champagne talking, isn't it?" she says.

"It is," I respond, smiling.

"What are you thinking you want to pay for the car?" the salesman asks. I instinctively know that, in this office, each and every day, prospective customers with finely refined senses of humor give hilarious answers like "Oh, 10 dollars" or "Maybe 100 bucks" or "About 1,000," to which the salesman responds with a wry chuckle and/or a friendly riposte like, "I wish I could do that." At this moment, I do not know whom to despise more for their role in this feeble burlesque, but it is an issue I will surely belabor with Greta later this evening.

Sidestepping the hackneyed exchange, I quote the salesman a figure. A handsome and entirely realistic sum that Greta and I arrived at on our test drive, before returning to the dealership. To our dismay, the salesman rejects it out of hand.

"No can do," he tells us. "Believe me, I know my sales manager and there's no way he's going to accept an offer in Swedish krona. Regardless of the exchange rate."

In an attempt to keep control of the negotiations, I make

another offer, this time in wheat futures. Again, we are re-buffed. Neither will our adversary consider a purchase in rare stamps, collectible kitsch, vials of semen from assorted Kentucky Derby champions, nor pollution credits.

"We're strictly dollars and cents here," the salesman advises us.

Greta, sensing (correctly) I'm about to seize on the salesman's ignorance of the world currency market and restate our desired purchase price in Zimbabwean dollars and cents, chooses this moment to enter the discussion and discloses to our adversary precisely how much we're willing to spend on the car in U.S. dollars. This, in my opinion, undermines our position, and I tell her so.

"I don't care about our position," she says. "We need a car. I want a car. I want *that* car."

Her words provoke two epiphanies in me. First, I realize that Greta, heedless of the explicit warnings contained in Power-Point slide twenty-four, has fallen in love with the car we're considering, thereby ensuring that, rather than being merely ripped off on the price, we'll endure a thorough, nonlubri-cated deflowering of our collective anal region. Second, I suddenly understand that, in the final analysis, overpaying for an automobile doesn't matter. What's important is that Greta, my dear sobbing, swollen-footed Greta, have everything she wants.

I relate to Greta what I've just realized and tell her we can buy the car for full sticker price, if that's what she genuinely wants.

I am immediately rewarded by an excited tittering, like that of a schoolgirl, followed by a warm, lingering kiss. These come, of course, from our salesman, who, after quickly writing up a purchase agreement for the full MSRP and obtaining my signature, goes off to find his sales manager in order to tell him he now believes in God.

Greta's reaction is, in her own way, equally effusive.

"I want to tell the whole world how you indulge me," she says. "But that would take far more phone calls than I have time for."

The sale is now complete. Which does not mean we are done. Or that we can leave. Instead, we are escorted by our salesman into the presence of an unexpected entity, a life unit he refers to simply as "the finance guy." This finance guy, we're told, is the person who will take our financial information (income, debt, credit limit, and assets, including all fully functional body organs), then arrange for, authorize, and approve our loan. He will shepherd our purchase to its true, final, and, we're assured, concluding conclusion, making sure all the i's are dotted, the t's crossed, the x's signed at or initialed next to, and the f's attached to the front of our "-uck me"'s.

My immediate impression of the man to whom we're introduced is that he *looks* like a finance guy, with the earnest attitude, fleshy physique, spacious walled-and-doored office, thick forms, and computing equipment one looks for in a finance guy. That I feel this way is odd since I've never before heard of, seen, or met a finance guy. In fact, as I think about it, I don't suppose I've ever met anyone associated with collecting large sums of money who has the noun "guy" in his job title, not a single mortgage guy, bank guy, IRS guy, or loan-sharking guy.

But a more surprising aspect of the finance guy is that— title be damned—he's not solely interested in finance. He's also interested in extending the sales process and increasing our fiscal obligation. It is his job to tempt us with products like a service warranty which extends our bumper-to-bumper coverage to other dimensions and parallel universes, title insurance (though this is withdrawn when it's discovered we're not members of the peerage), a "floating deed" that gives us the mineral rights to any parking space we happen to be occupying at a given time, and a transferable whole life insurance policy that will cover any fighting cock we might transport in the trunk carrier.

Greta and I, knowing the purchase price of the car has taken us to the very edge of our credit limit, decline these new and additional enticements as unaffordable. Not so, we're told. The current amount of our loan would have us *swimming* in debt; the finance company has approved us to *drown* in it, meaning we still have several thousand dollars before being cut off. Flattered and encouraged by the lender's confidence, we opt to purchase: an original William Wegman photo of a Weimaraner behind the wheel of our new car; PreDing®, a small, unobtrusive dent installed by the dealership's service department, thereby relieving new car owners of the anxiety associated with trying to keep their vehicle in pristine condition; and, because one can never go wrong with real estate, the floating deed.

Between his sales efforts and the multitudinous agreements, contracts, applications, releases, waivers, and vouchers he has us (profess to) read, then fill out and sign, the finance guy holds us captive for over two-and-a-half hours. By session's end, Greta and I are drained, sagging; he looks fresh as a cardboard cutout.

"Okay" he says, "if I can just get you to sign this last form, you can be on your way. All this is, is a waiver stating that, in exchange for signing this waiver, you waive all legal claims against the dealership as a result of being exposed to the several known carcinogens used in the printing of this waiver."

We sign.

"That's it, "the finance guy says. Across the desk, he hands us each our own a set of car keys. "Congratulations."

"It's ours now?" Greta asks. "We own it?"

"Yes," he says. "The car's all yours."

We both sigh with relief, grateful to be done with this difficult process. Standing to leave, I feel empty in areas other than my pockets, specifically, my scrotum, since, in an instinctive act of self-preservation, my testicles undescended hours ago. Greta, I notice, looks equally spent in her own way. We shuffle from the finance guy's office, pass through the showroom, and push through the front door into the cool evening air. Our car, newly washed and shining, awaits. Before we get in, I turn and wrap Greta in a deep embrace.

"Thank God that's over," I whisper into her ear.

And in mine she whispers back, "Well, it is until I get the tinted contacts I'm thinking about."

Greta drives us off the lot, steers us toward home. We are car owners now—again—like so much of America. Speeding down the highway, I suddenly become aware of the specters of obesity, highway fatalities, and global warming securely seat-belted into the spacious back seat. Ah, well.

"Are you happy?" I ask.

"I'm not unhappy," she says.

"Good. Then I'm not unhappy, too."

We ride for a moment in silence, both utterly and completely not unhappy.

Then, "Do you hear that rattle?"

24 } Minor (Under 18) Damage

I'm not entirely comfortable around kids. I'm even less comfortable around education. "Then why in the world," a reasonable person might ask, "would you volunteer to be a mentor?"

"Well," I'd inform this reasonable person with the impertinence I could live without, "I feel a societal obligation to wise up at least one little *pisher* on a few items he won't find in his schoolbooks but which are far more essential to a happy life than memorizing *The Something of Whatzit* by Guy With a Quill Pen or remembering when DeSoto discovered the tailfin. Specifically, these items are: 1. Work hard in school and people will expect you to work hard the rest of your goddamned life. 2. There's no such thing as a *small* pimple. 3. If you don't make a bowling pin lamp in Shop class, you'll never stop kicking yourself in the ass. 4. You may think you have friends, but when the chips are down and you ask a bud to sell his car and give you the money to score a pound of bomb weed to deal so you'll have enough cash to split for California, you'll find that the word "friend" is a hollow, meaningless sham.

The application the school had me fill out asked a lot of personal questions. Questions I wasn't altogether willing to answer. Like, "Name?" and "Zip Code?" So I fudged my answers. And I guess I did a pretty good job, because the next week, when I interviewed with Ms. Kugel, the head of the mentoring program, the first thing out of her mouth was, "You know, you just *look* like someone named Dr. Zoltan of the Jungle."

The rest of the interview went just as swimmingly. Toward the end, she told me I was exactly the kind of candidate her desperately-short-of-resources/desperately-short-of-mentors mentor program needed: I had no history of sexual predation, possessed the kind of free time successful people didn't have to give, and indicated an indifference to the possibility of head lice.

Not long after this, I got my assignment, my protégé: one Derek Spivey. Frankly, looking over the profile Ms. Kugel had sent me, I was rather disappointed.

First, Derek was thirteen years old. I'd really wanted a younger student—first grade, tops—so that I could make an immediate and immense impact on his/her incipient identity. It seemed to me that having a significant influence on a teenager's life would necessitate powerful psychotropics and a Vietcong tiger cage, one of which I sure as hell wasn't willing to waste on some punk.

Strike two: Derek was white. I'd been hoping for a child of color because I felt s/he'd better accessorize the earth tones that dominate my wardrobe. Finally, rather than Derek's father being the family-deserting deadbeat I'd expected, the damn guy was just *dead*. Deceased. In-the-ground bound. Meaning the boy probably had "grief issues," or, as I thought of them, "sissy-crying-baby bullshit." Plus, I'd been fairly confident, even a little cocky, about how I'd stack up next to a highly resented, good-for-nothing absentee parent, but next to a mourned Daddykins? How could I compete with that?

Bottom line was, I was completely screwed. Screwed by some over-the-hill whimpering white bookworm with a hole in his life. Well, fuck *me*.

All that being said, after long reflection, I decided to take Derek on. What can I say? I'm all about people.

I called Derek's house and got his mom. I explained who I was and asked to speak with the boy. She said he was busy doing homework (here's a kid *screaming* for Life Lesson #1, I told myself) but she'd go get him.

He sounded like a nice enough kid. Clever. A little shy. We talked for a bit and arranged to meet the next day at his school, after last bell. When he asked how he'd recognize me, I told him, "I'll be the guy who looks like he'd go well with browns."

A mentor, it turns out, has three basic responsibilities: setting an overall example for the child; offering support and guidance; and helping with schoolwork. In the first two areas, I was exemplary, equal parts Oprah and Lassie. Honestly, after the first week, I felt so confident about the job I was doing, I found out where Derek's father's was buried just so I could drop by and tell him, "In your face!"

The last item, though, the schoolwork thing, proved thorny. Derek needed help in U.S. Geography and Math. And though I'd been uncharacteristically truthful on the application when I said these were my "strong subjects," there had been no room to clarify that, out of respect for the indigenous people of this continent, not only do I deny the legitimacy of the so-called fifty "states," but I refuse to recognize the borders or names given them by the white European invaders and their descendents, as well as all cities, landforms, and landmarks contained within them; I was also shocked and dismayed to learn that Derek's school was using the word "Math" as a colloquialism for "Mathematics" rather than "Jerry 'The Beaver' Mathers."

But I'd come too far to turn back now. I was enjoying Derek's company. I found him to be fresh, eager, and my ticket of legitimacy for getting into the gym to watch after-school varsity cheerleader practice. So, rather than admit my shortcomings, I decided to fake my way through the educational aspect of the mentoring program. After all, I reasoned, Derek's a thirteen-year-old who's underachieving in the very classes I'm supposed to help with, how hard can it be to buffalo him into thinking I've got all the answers?

My instincts proved to be correct. Derek was anxious to learn everything his new buddy and mentor told him. And while I absolutely shoulder the blame for teaching him the highest peak in America is Mt. Endew and that parallelograms are two telegrams sent at the same time, certainly the boy must bear some responsibility for being so gullible as to believe, no matter how vehemently I may have insisted, that Snottysnotville is the capital of Mucuschusetts and the answer to all quadratic equations is "X^{CUSE} M$^{\text{E?}}$."

But regardless of who is or isn't the culpable party here, it's Derek whose grades suffered. Over the three weeks we worked and studied together, his test scores dropped by an average of 10,497%. At least by my calculations. Thankfully, grade inflation kept his final class marks at the "A" level.

Once it was clear to Derek, however, that I was deficient in the areas in which he needed help and that I was okay with him remaining the unfortunate victim of that, he got upset. So upset, in fact, he went to Ms. Kugel and insisted on a different mentor. She complied. To his credit though, he had the guts to "fire" me personally.

"I'm sorry, Dr. Zoltan of the Jungle," he said, polite to the end, "I need a *smart* mentor."

Ouch. That hurt. But I understood. I really did. That's why, when I paid the school bully twenty bucks to beat Derek up, I told him to lay off the face.

25 } Holy Roller Coaster

My instinct was to say no. In fact, I did say no. But I said it wrong, tried to be too diplomatic. What I told him on the phone was this: "I don't know if I'm the right person to go with you to Dollywood."

As soon as it hit air, I knew I'd blown it.

"Bob, *I* think you're the right person to go and, remember, I'm infallible." And so I was stuck meeting Pope John Paul II in Pigeon Forge, Tennessee.

We'd arranged to meet right inside the main gate. And sure enough, when I arrived, there he was waiting for me. Alone. (Central Tennessee being an adamantly Baptist/fundamentalist enclave, swarming autograph hounds and ring kissers *weren't* an issue.) It was an unusually hot, humid day in the foothills, but thankfully Deuce (as friends call him) was sporting his summer vestments—short sleeves, knee-length cassock (all breathable 100 percent cotton), flip-flops, and, in place of his regular topper, a blinding-white sun visor with understated gold brocade and inlaid gems.

"Hot enough for ya?" I said, by way of a greeting.

"Hell's bells," he answered, "I've issued encyclicals condemning Third World tyrants who've been less oppressive than this heat."

Okay. Let me go on record right now and say I think Deuce is a helluva funny guy, but sometimes he tries a little too hard.

* * *

I asked him what he wanted to do first. He said the Vatican buzz was all about Daredevil Falls but he didn't want to get wet so early in the day.

"You up for the Tennessee Tornado?" he asked.

"Depends," I said. "When the coaster pulls back in the station are you going to make a spectacle of yourself and kiss the platform?"

"Hey, it's what I do," he said.

"Let's start with the carousel then."

"You're about as much fun as an Act of Contrition," he groused.

Great, I thought, we've been here two minutes and already I'm getting attitude. If we make it through this day without a major blow-up it'll be a miracle. Though, of course, whether it's officially designated as such won't be *my* call.

After a few rides, as we were slouching toward Daydream Ridge (damn if I didn't wish he'd thought to bring his PopeMoCart electric scooter; it took us *forever* to walk from area to area), I mentioned to Deuce that I was getting hungry.

"I could eat a couple chilidogs," he said, which, besides the occasional body and blood of Christ, I swear, is all I've ever seen the man eat.

So we wait in line, and I order. It's not until we get the total that—surprise!—he's forgotten to change his lire for dollars and I'm stuck for the whole shebang. He offers me a couple of indulgences to cover his share.

"Those and two million lire'll get me a cup of coffee," I mutter.

Pissing him off yet *again*. To the extent that he stretches out grace for over a frigging hour, in Latin, and by the time he's done the chilidogs are soggy and tepid. Inedible.

"The Turk who shot you, he gets forgiven. Me, I get vindictiveness," I grumbled.

An inscrutable grin spread his thin lips, "Yin and yang, Bob," he says, "yin and yang."

Late in the afternoon, the Pope's energy sagged. Too much sun and excitement and standing in line, I guess.

"What say we do some people watching?" I suggested.

We commandeered a bench under a shady tree and sat quietly. But Deuce is a restless type and before long he'd concocted a game to entertain himself. Snap Damnation, he called it. What he'd do is single out a park patron and, for whatever reason— "Get some clothes on, harlot;" "Look how the crying boy dishonors his parents;" "Tell me *she* hasn't had an abortion"—he'd condemn him/her, right then and there, to an eternity in Hell. Awfully judgmental, I thought, but, whatever, when with the Bishop of Rome…

After twenty minutes, though, bored with his shtick, I reminded him, "Totally pointless, dawg. They're not even Catholic."

He countered with mock indignation, "Well, just flog my fun through the streets and nail it to a cross on a hill, why don't you?" Still trying too hard, yes, but jeez, how do you *not* laugh?

Nightfall. And Deuce's age and Parkinson's had caught up to him. He was so bent over he'd started falling short of the "you must be taller than this" cartoon cutouts at the "big people" rides. It was time to go home.

"I had fun," he said, arching his eyebrows expectantly. "You?"

26 } Bang! You're Did.

The decision to get the shaft of my penis pierced wasn't made overnight. I discussed it with my girlfriend, my family, my clergyman, my shrink, my mechanic, the pizza delivery guy, and Dr. Laura. All of them were against it. Which is fine. I really just wanted to talk about the shaft of my penis.

For the unperforated, I don't recommend the genitalia as a first pierce. Unh-unh. The first time you see a twenty-something minimum-wager with a buzz cut, skin the color of a snowcap mushroom, XXL Rage Against the Machine T-shirt, and painted black fingernails coming at you with a spring-loaded needle gun, you'll definitely want him aiming above your waist. Maybe at your ears. Or a nostril. Me? I'm more riddled with holes than a Chinese checkers board; pierced top to bottom—eyebrows, lips and tongue, full ear perimeter, septum, nipples, navel, toe-webbing, and prefrontal lobe (though, technically, that last one was more of a nail gun accident).

My feeling was that for a procedure as sensitive as a shaft job, I should go with a specialist. No way did I want to get my most valuable plumbing skewered and wind up peeing at ninety degrees from straight south (a real possibility according to the "bible of studcraft," *The Hole Truth*). That meant my regular old "Pop 'n' Go" studding parlor was out, and the little penile boutique I'd spotted near campus, "Members Only," was in.

* * *

Sometimes, late at night, when it's really quiet, I lay in bed and wonder why I'm so drawn to piercing. The best I've been able to do is narrow the reasons to four: 1. Low skin esteem; 2. A love for seriously backing things up at the airport metal detector; 3. A potassium deficiency; 4. How totally cool my face looks as I'm yelling, *"Yeeeooooooooooooooow!"*

The Members Only staff was undeniably upscale: nails buffed to a high gloss, their Ts fresh-off-the-silk-screener fresh, and instead of Taco Bell bags and wrappers and cups laying around everywhere, they were almost all stuffed into a battered garbage can. Overall, the atmosphere was less dark, less aloof than I was used to, too, but not way so. Kind of like going to the movies expecting to see a David Lynch film but getting a Kubrick one instead. As I stood waiting to be helped, I glanced at the thick deck of business cards on the counter, near the cash register. Under the boutique's embossed logo was their slogan: "Hold *very* still."

Some people ask, "Did you think about what effect this kind of piercing would have on your sex life?" I tell them, "I am a male human between the ages of birth and death—I think about what effect high humidity will have on my sex life."

I thought there'd be one standard take-it-or-leave-it penis stud, but I was wrong. They had stainless steel balls of all diameters, wire hoops, symbols, gemstones, Disney characters, even corporate logos, from the Nike "Swoosh" to "Nathan's Famous." I chose one that was marked down for quick sale, a small enameled disc with the words, "If you can read this, you're not quite close enough."

The only problem I foresaw with this piercing was that it would be seen by less of the public than my other ones. After all, I'm not a male hustler, porno star, flasher, locker room denizen, nudist, or Boston priest. Still, I knew I'd want to show it off. Then it hit me: where is it written that you can only Xerox your *ass* at the office?

"Go-time" had arrived. And I have to admit that as many times as I've been punctured, I never felt so vulnerable, so self-conscious, so uncertain, as I did standing there, shorts around ankles, the Head Piercer (his title, not his job description, I was happy to find out) surveying my "situation." "Time to make the donuts," he said, semicryptically. I heard a tissue-deadened "pop" and, for a second, I felt nothing. Then, for a period of time when the clocks stopped and the sun turned to ice, I thoroughly felt 100 percent of totally all of everything ever.

With piercing, it's all about what's next? To which I have only one word to say: Uvula.

27 } Geek Noir

It was late. Heinously late. A pitch-black time of night better suited to vampires and vampire slayers, owls and owl slayers. But there *I* was. Still at it. Burning the midnight kilowatt-hours. Don't get me wrong, though. I'm not complaining. It's all part of the job. Like I always say, when you're a PI(IS)— Private Investigator (Internet Specialist)—the workdays are longer than Yao Ming's inseam.

As usual, I'd killed the office overheads, which left me working in the cool, gunmetal-blue glow of my flat panel display. The Feds—those lousy OSHA bulls—frowned on this little habit of mine. Said my arrangement caused "eyestrain." Verbally warned me. Twice. What they don't get is that I don't like being leaned on. Never have. So I keep on cutting the candlepower *as* I want, *when* I want. And if the flatfoots should decide they want to play hardball, well, they'll find out this is one Web Dick tough enough to take any written citation they can dish out.

The little matter I had my sleeves rolled up on that night was a missing person case—which in the business are called "doe sluts" because, generally speaking, there's "lotsa bucks in 'em." My client, a forty-something bag of wrinkled meat, wanted me to poke around online and see if I could turn up the drill team dish he didn't have the *cajones* to ask out in high school and hadn't seen since graduation in '79. As usual in the Internet side of Private Investigation, no foul play was suspected in the case. It also didn't figure she was hiding or that she'd disappeared on purpose; she'd probably just gotten on with her life. Not that that made my job any easier. Especially since all I had to go on was a (maiden?) name and a twenty-two-year-old address. I'd been chasing leads all day, doing the "glamorous" sitting-on-your-ass legwork that most mugs don't realize is 99.99999999993 percent of an e-tective's job.

The going had been slow at first. My usually reliable dot-coms, dot-orgs, dot-govs, dot-edus, and dot-nets had turned up dot-squat. Time dragged. Then, just after midnight, I'd picked up a fresh scent, and, *bam*, I was off, nose to the trail, ass to the world. The chatter of my ergonomic keyboard and the triple-quick clicks of my trackball made more clackety racket than a Siamese Savion Glover with a crystal meth monkey on his back. I was locked on and in hot pursuit. It was in the heat of this surge that I heard:

"Excuse me? I'm looking for a Mr. Cody Airrer."

What with my mad concentration and the din from my dogged digits, I was taken totally by surprise. But I've been at this dodge long enough to know better than to show it. I kept right on keying, cool as the last bowl of gazpacho at a South Pole Cinco de Mayo celebration. After a few seconds, I stopped and flexed my knuckles, triggering more pops than a Glock; only then did I unstick my eyeballs from the screen and shift them in the direction of the voice.

What I saw, standing there in the doorway of my cubicle, was a vision. Something a gumchew like me can only read about, dream about, or see in two dimensions on 3.16 million porn sites. That is to say, I was looking at an actual, in-the-flesh female person. And she was close. Less than a ten-foot pole close. All of a sudden, I was hot as a CPU with a faulty internal fan housing. Of course, she didn't need to know that.

"Airrer found," I said flatly, though, in my head, I was mad high-five-ing myself for accessing such a slammin' comeback on the spur. "And the office is closed. More to the point, it's a virtual office, so it's *always* closed to in-person visits. *Call* in the morning."

I thought maybe the dame was deaf because she breezed right into my space, ignoring my good advice as well as the threatening sound chip snarl she'd triggered from my AIBO dogbot (that was 1,500 bucks down the crapper). My peepers followed her. She came to a stop in front of my monitor and stood there, blocking the flat-screen with her 17.2-inch measured diagonally (but who was measuring in that direction?) caboose. My semi-slack jaw told her she had my attention.

"I'm desperate, Mr. Airrer," she said. "I'll do *anything* if you'll help me."

I liked the sound of that. I mean, it doesn't take a cyber-sleuth to know desperation is just a date waiting to happen.

She stood there, waiting for my answer, wondering if I'd agree to help her. I wondered, too.

The reason I shouldn't get involved was obvious: I got into the Private i-Investigation racket to interface with computers, not people. On the other hand, I had the distinct feeling that if I turned this do-anything doll down, she might lose it, go ballistic, maybe take it out on my hardware. And how would I explain *that* to corporate?

While I chewed things over, I looked my visitor up and down. She was different than a lot of dames. Petite, but not fragile. Cute, but not as a button. Older (thirty, maybe thirty-two), but holding her own against gravity (though I may have caught a whiff of Replenisher with Retinol). Altogether, she was some package. Real FedEx material: the kind of hottie I absolutely, positively wanted to be there with me overnight.

I was done chewing and ready to swallow.

"Take the load off," I said, brushing some Subway lunch litter off a stack of *Wired* back issues so she'd have a place to park her keister. "And drop the 'Mr. Airrer' bit. The name's Cody. But everyone calls me Code."

"As in Zip?" she purred.

"As in lines of, source, binary, bar, programming, Windows, Unix, malicious, et cetera. I could go on but why don't you just Google it later instead," I replied. I pulled a cigarette from the pack on my desk, put it in my mouth, and didn't light up (this is a No Smoking building). "Besides, you're not here to talk about name origins. There's something else taxing your hard drive. So come on, spill it. And try to keep it short. Lots of cutting, no pasting."

"Okay. Sure." I'd ruffled her feathers but this bird wasn't flying anywhere; she'd just whistle her tune through a clenched—and perfectly lipsticked—beak. "A few weeks ago, I inherited a considerable sum of money. *Very* considerable. I wanted to invest it but didn't know in what. So, while I looked over various options, I parked the money in the bank. In the passbook account I shared with my husband."

I knew where this was going. It was a story older than UNI-VAC.

"Then, last Thursday morning, I woke up to find a note from my husband on the kitchen table. He said he was going away, far away, and doing it on the money from our joint account. When I called the bank, they said my account balance was zero."

"And you want me to recover your dough."

She nodded.

I opened my bottom right desk drawer and took out a half-full can of Red Bull and a Styrofoam cup. I offered a drink to the lady.

She shook her head. "I'm afraid high caffeine drinks go straight to my heart and cause unpleasant palpitations," she said.

I put the cup back and took a long pull of Bull right from the can. "I'll take your case," I told her. Then added: "My fee is an $89.95 minimum for up to two hours plus expenses, after the first two hours my rate is $35/hour in quarter hour increments. It's all outlined in this contract which you'll have to sign here...and initial here ...and here...and I'll need a major credit card. For a deposit."

She did as she was told.

"There's just one more thing," I said, waiting for authorization on her Visa.

"What's that?"

"I'll need your hubby's SS."

She showed no response. Nothing. It was like she was the general public and I was one of Kevin Costner's last six movies.

"His *Social Security number,*" I explained. "You got it?"

She did. I went to work.

Things got off to a fast start, went my way. I was on the move, in the flow, flying higher than a Global Positioning Satellite. Then, from out of nowhere, *boom.* There was a crash.

"God*damn* this machine," I shouted. "'Fatal error?' What'd I do? This is the third time it's crashed today. I gotta reboot..."

After I was back up and running, I fell right back in the groove. Having the SS number and knowing how to hack into the computer systems of most large American banks made it a piece of flan to find the bandito and the dinero. With a few quick keystrokes—*powpowpow*—I transferred the jack back into her account. Then, because hubby was a lowlife scuzz who deserved it, I opened a CitiBank credit card in his name and used it to order the latest *Grand Theft Auto, Unreal Tournament 2004, Half-Life 2,* and a couple of other titles for myself.

"All set," I informed her.

"That's it, Code? Just some typing on a computer? No skulking in dark alleys? No dead ends or red herrings? No rough stuff?"

"The only rough stuff this PI(IS) runs into is when the mail boy occasionally calls me a 'fucking nerd asshole,'" I said. "It's a new day, sweetheart. A new world."

She looked disappointed. Crestfallen. I could see there'd be no Love Connection tonight. Hell, a pepper-sprayed blind man could see that. "Guess if I want hardboiled," she sighed, "I'll just have to wait for my Easter basket."

Easter, I thought. Isn't that what my parents used to call Spring Break? I made a mental note to ask them about that when we were instant messaging later. But right now, there was a big fat messy loose end to wrap up.

"Do you want to keep that on your Visa?" I asked, pointedly.

"That works," was her cool reply.

"Look, lady, I don't need you getting all disillusioned on me about this," I said. "Times change. Methods change. Job titles, classifications, and descriptions as issued by the U.S. Department of Labor change." She didn't look convinced, won over. But so what. I didn't give a damn what she thought. You know, so long as she didn't trash me on a Customer Comment card and get management all up in my face.

28 } Love is One of the Answers

"I can't figure it out," a friend said to me the other afternoon. "Sometimes it feels serious, other times I think we're winding down." She was referencing her current relationship. The guy she's dating. *Been* dating. For five months. Which is why her uncertainty completely baffled me. In an effort to help her clarify matters, I carefully formulated and asked three penetrating questions: Was it really possible—after so much time—that she honestly didn't know how things stood? *Really, really* possible? *Really, really, really* possible? She answered, "Yes" to all three questions.

This got me thinking: As someone who's had a number of serious relationships ("serious" being defined as, "eventually having to get lawyers involved"), I'm well-acquainted with the subtleties of love. Perhaps I could be of some assistance to my friend. And to others like her. So, through insights gained by my own experience and in the hope that it will help uncertain lovers to evaluate the true depth of their relationships, I put together the following quiz.

We share a lot of the same interests, like:
- a. Ummm...
- b. Uhhh...
- c. Hmmm...
- d. Er...let's see...um, don't tell me...uh...well, um, we did that, uh, thing, um, last summer, I think...

Our relationship would be absolutely perfect if we could be with each other:

    a. Every day.

    b. Every week.

    c. Every February 29.

Rank the following intimate activities as indicators of a serious relationship, starting with the most significant:

    a. Showing each other your drivers license photos.

    b. Having sober sex.

    c. Choosing a vacation destination regardless of its extradition policy.

    d. Farting freely in a closed car.

When we want to celebrate a special occasion, like an anniversary or birthday, and we go out to a quiet, romantic dinner, my lover always:

    a. Makes the reservation for three, then, upon arriving, instructs the maitre d' to send over any hot single who might come in.

    b. "Forgets" to bring any cash or a credit card.

    c. Facilitates service by wearing shoes and shirt.

    d. Demands to know why they no longer use the funny little talking Chihuahua in their ads.

I'm more inclined to:

    a. Comfort my sweetheart with a lie.

    b. Flog my sweetheart with the truth.

Agree or disagree:

    A partner consumed by desire is likely to be regurgitated?

In an argument, I'm always the first to:
   a. Apologize insincerely so we can just *fucking* get on with our *fucking* lives, all right?
   b. Recount the tragic ending of *Old Yeller* in an attempt to radically alter the mood, then move in for the kill on my emotionally weakened adversary.
   c. Rail against the five-day waiting period restricting my Second Amendment rights.

Until I met my lover I thought I'd go my whole life without:
   a. Achieving a convincing fake orgasm.
   b. Achieving a convincing fake identity.
   c. Becoming gay.

True or false:
In order for any relationship to grow and flower one partner must accept the role of fertilizer?

Looking into my lover's eyes, I see:
   a. Eye boogers.
   b. Lucid gems of molten passion that immerse me in the heat of a million suns, inciting each of my very cells to vibrate with a sensation of half pain, half pleasure as I ride the glass-scaled spine of the vermilion dragon toward the tiger-stalked forests of Valhalla where ohmygod, baby, are you gettin' off on this X like I am...?
   c. Hair. (If you chose c., you're *behind* your lover; circle around to the front and look again)

We've talked about children and agree that:

    a. They're small.

    b. They can't handle their liquor.

    c. George and Barbara Bush shouldn't have had any.

I often fantasize about my lover in:

    a. A tight, brief bathing suit.

    b. A Jenny Craig program.

    c. Harm's way.

When it comes to brains:

    a. I usually beat my mate at Jeopardy.

    b. My mate usually beats me at Jeopardy.

    c. We'd both like to beat Alex Trebek's out.

Politically speaking:

    a. We both believe that the major party candidates are an insult to voters and an embarrassment to the democratic process.

    b. All of the above.

If my lover were to suddenly leave me, I would:

    a. Almost certainly notice.

    b. Dig out the ol' "roofies" prescription.

    c. Not tell my spouse.

SCORING: Count up all your answers. Multiply by the number of wives Larry King has had, then divide by the number of spam emails for Viagra you've received this week. Show the number to your lover. If s/he glances at it then tells you your answer is wrong, you're definitely in a serious relationship.

29 } Sawdust Memories

My lover and I go to the circus every time it comes to town. I because I'm enchanted by the ballet-slippered nymph who stands on the bare back of the serious white stallion as he gallops round the center ring; my lover because she despises the same woman (both for her grace and her skill) and hopes to be there the night she takes a crippling, career-ending fall.

And so, once again, ultimately, the circus will be fun for only one of us.

We sit in darkness. "Lay-dies and gen-tell-men," the ringmaster crows from his lonely spot of light, "behold the splen-door, the gran-door of the Pah-rade of Staaaaars." With a wave of his hand, the big top is instantly bathed in brilliant brightness. Revealed is the entire troupe—every acrobat, artiste, clown, animal, and trainer—circling the floor's perimeter, passing the stands for review. All of them—remarkably!—walking in reverse. When I comment on this exceptional feat, my lover tells me my contact lenses are in backwards.

Though gaily dressed, the clowns are a disappointment. Instead of amusing their audience with acts of buffoonery, they explain to us—at length and with the aid of overheads and handouts—the theory, historical context, and psychology of finding humor in the exaggerated and preposterous behavior of others. Later, I read in the program that these merry-andrews are not only graduates of Clown College, but also of Clown Grad School.

Our collective attention is directed to a fine and fearless couple ninety feet above the sawdust floor. They dazzle us with their mastery of high-wire walking. Astonish us with some high wire-rope-skipping. Astound us with high-wire bicycling. Begin to lose us with high-wire juggling. Exasperate us with high-wire Texas Hold 'Em playing. And eventually, earn our contempt with high-wire tax accounting, high-wire Web page designing, high-wire accepting a package from UPS, high-wire tire rotation, and high-wire wireless phone calling.

The bawl of the wild jungle cats. The ripplingly muscled young men in sequins. The dizzying potpourri of barked commands, swirling hot lights, and musky scents. Why am I suddenly reminded of the curious weekend I spent with Siegfried & Roy all those years ago?

In the third ring stands an enormous cannon, its barrel long as a train car, its bore broad as a man's shoulders. But instead of the Human Cannonball we expect, the ringmaster introduces Charlton Heston, who comes out and gives a short talk on how Congressional Democrats want to take away an individual's right to own this gun, even though it's used mostly for hunting.

Everything under the big top fills me with much wonder. A wonder that spawns large questions. Like: What are the physical limitations of the human body? Does superior intelligence make man the master of all beasts or their caretakers?

Should a hot dog have a skeleton?

The ballet-slippered angel performs flawlessly, captivating the audience. Then, just as she's finishing her act, at a most critical and precarious moment, I draw an air horn from my coat pocket and give a loud, long blast. The stallion flinches. The girl falters. Pitches forward. Falls beneath thundering hooves. Ligaments snap. With the sound of harp strings.

My lover kisses my cheek. Calls me a romantic. She would know.

30 } Uniform Traditions

The ballyhoo is irresistible. For weeks it builds in the stores, then, slowly, it takes over the streets. The decorations, the songs, the merriment become ubiquitous. Before you know it—before you're ready?—you're merrily trading gifts with the family, toasting with old friends, drunkenly cheering a drunken fight between ex-sailors and ex-marines in the parking lot of the VFW hall. Then, suddenly, it's over. Finished. The calendar coldly informs us it's November 12th. Back to normal. Another Veterans Day has come and too quickly gone. And once again, fond memories of this sweet season for warrior patriots must sustain us until the next.

My first memories of Veterans Day stretch back to early childhood. My father, a proud Army draftee of 1942 and WWII vet, would take me downtown to see the impressive displays of armaments and ordnance. The street corner dogfaces, decked in camouflage and combat boots, would be stationed next to their red, white, and blue kettles ardently appealing to passersby to donate ammunition to send to the poor American kids—the very future of the VFW—fighting in the jungles of Vietnam. Dad was a soft touch and always gave more clips than we could afford. "Believe me," he once counseled, "those care packages of bullets from home mean a lot to a kid overseas at war. They remind you of what you're fighting for." A quiet moment passed, then he added, "No, that's wrong. I mean, 'fighting with.'"

After lunch (in those days, special holiday "shit on a shingle" carts dotted the sidewalks, and we'd always eat at one; my preference for the shingles and a tendency toward precociousness always led me to pipe in, "One with light shit, please, sir"), we'd go to one of the big department stores and Dad would march me through Martin-Marietta's Wonderful Weaponry Workshop. Every year, I'd stagger wide-eyed and slack-jawed through this fantastic world of $6,000 toilet seats and $800 hammers. Of magical, marvelous warheads that could decimate populations yet spare the infrastructure. Of then-futuristic fancies like night vision and Stealth technology and lasers and palatable field rations. It was here, in the WWW, that I realized, on some instinctive, nonverbal level, that the budding Computer Age was going to make bombing civilizations back to the Stone Age a lot easier.

As you might expect, at the end of the Workshop tour was a doorway. A doorway with a long line of children. All anxiously waiting, of course, to be escorted into General Ulysses S. Grant's Office. There, just like kids today, we climbed on the old boy's lap and told him what we wanted the Congress to budget for the Department of Defense in the coming year. (I remember these roly-poly "Grant's Helpers" of my youth as dead ringers for the old boy, right down to the flask bulge and whiskey breath.) And how could I not believe in the General when, no matter how high or ridiculous a dollar figure I named, DOD appropriations were always that much and "a few ten thousand million more?"

These days, I tend to wait until the last minute to do my

Veterans Day shopping. Somehow it feels more authentic, more like combat, to be out amongst the anxious, desperate, purchasing hordes. Of course, the crowds of today are not downtown but at suburban malls. Where, lamentably, some of the more fanciful touches of the old department stores are missing. Still, I get a tingle of anticipation when I go through the doors of my local buy-o-sphere and see the promenade all decked in its holiday khaki, sprinkled with merry accents of olive drab, dress blue, and dress white. I delight in the retailers' replacement of their walkthrough shoplifting detectors with Checkpoint Charlie exit stops where bags of purchases are run through with bayonets or confiscated. I'm a sucker for the corny-but-charming Jimmy, the Jut-Jawed Joint Chief life-size animated figure, the traditional Boot Camp crèche, and the pungent seasonal aromas of cavalry and napalm.

But, really, it's the little, unexpected things—like an aging quartet of Korean War vets harmonizing on the theme from *M*A*S*H* ("Suicide Is Painless") in the atrium or a group of kids playing a pick-up game of Frag the Louie in the Food Court—that really get to me. It's just such "unforeseens" that can truly transform a "de-militarized zone" into a magical, enchanted—*but definitely not "fairy-"*—land.

I know I can't get caught up in the decorations and booby-trappings of the holidays indefinitely, though. There's shopping to be done. It's time to suck it up, storm the stores, and capture a few items for the brave soldiers-past and -present on my shopping list.

For Dad, I score a copy of Tom Brokaw's latest, *The Greatest Generation: Reflections on Putting Up with Subsequent, Inferior Generations*. It's the fifth year in a row I've bought a "Greatest

Generation"-themed book for him, but that's okay because it's become pretty clear that he and his fellow Axis-kickers can't get enough of themselves. For my uncle Paul, who served in Vietnam, there's no question: a classic Zig-Zags & Dime Bag gift box set. Blake, my cut-up cousin who fought in Operation Desert Storm, gets a gag gift: a framed "letter" from the Pentagon admitting the existence of, and their culpability in, Gulf War Syndrome. Ha-ha. Finally, for my niece, Steph, an Air Force Academy grad and Gulf War II vet, I pick up a gift certificate for rape counseling.

As the big day approaches, family and family tradition become the focus. For me and mine, that means on Veterans Day Eve, we all head down to the VFW for the ceremonial lighting of the peacenik (one year, Mom, herself an ex-WAVE, had the honor of dousing him in kerosene). Next, the whole membership forms a circle for a solemn, candlelit Denial of Atrocities ceremony. Afterwards, the energy level ticks up several notches as everyone troops inside the hall for a PX-travagant feast of long neck Buds, BBQ potato chips, and unfiltered cigarettes, followed by a game of nickel-dime poker that lasts till 2 or 3 A.M. Damn if it isn't just like a Norman Rockwell painting.

The next morning—Veterans Day day—always plays out the same way. The whole house is up before reveille. Creeping downstairs on our bellies, we soon spy telltale signs that the Special Forces Commando Unit has been here, rappelling down the side of the house from the rooftop, smashing through the windows, and leaving gifts for all good vets (that is, *all* vets, *period*). After the opening of the gifts and double-timing it three times around the backyard's perimeter, the family confabs in the kitchen for breakfast (powdered eggs) and Dad's annual reading of "A Visit from Old Ike" (or, as most of us know it, "'Twas the Night Before D-Day"). Perfect.

The rest of the day? Pretty subdued. We watch the parades and, on ESPN Classic, the Army-Navy games of 1962, 1969, and 1974. The kids do normal kid stuff, gorge themselves silly on Gingerbread Jarhead cookies, shoot 'friendly-fire' spit wads at each other, and trade shouts of "worthless maggot" till everyone's self is sublimated to the group. Adults and children alike are in their racks by 7:30 P.M. All-in. Sorry to see another Veterans Day pass so quickly. The only consolation is that in less than a month there'll be Pearl Harbor Day to celebrate.

31 } No. Thank *You.*

Heavenly Father, we thank You for this Thanksgiving bounty which we are about to receive. We ask You to bless this lovingly prepared turkey and, in the process, to neutralize the effects of its mind-fogging tryptophan, Satan's evil turkey narcotic. Please bless both our dressings—that within the bird's gutted cavity as well as that without; our yams as well as our mashed; our chunky whole-berry cranberry sauce along with our jellied slices; and, of course, your Holy Trinity of pies: the tart apple, the mellow pumpkin, and the sweet pecan. Yea, and we beseech Thee, O Omnipotent God, in Your infinite mercy, to render our gravy lumpless in order that we might have no reason to gag upon it and rain blows upon Aunt Louise.

Also, Almighty Lord, allow me now, while our heads are bowed, to express this family's everlasting appreciation for the many, many gifts You've seen fit to heap upon us since last we prayed out loud over any meal featuring giblets. Because truly we benefit from Your generosity daily. And on a good day, hourly.

I only have to see great-grandma Schmedwin seated at table once again this year to be reminded of how fortunate we all are to have been granted another year in the company of her life-affirming spirit. As You know, All-knowing Redeemer, the fall feast would not be the same without the sight of this saintly woman sleeping facedown in her overflowing dinner plate. We humbly ask that Thee be merciful with this elder and slow the progress of her crippling hump though we in no way question why You visited it upon her in the first place.

I thank You, too, Heavenly Keeper-Safer, for delivering my oldest daughter Rita from the radical religious cult she'd fallen in with while away at Bob Jones University. With Your help and the deprogrammer's vigilance, Mother and I are most confident she'll never again return to the dark practices and profane rituals of Presbyterianism.

My little brother, Herb, and his wife wish me to proclaim their eternal gratitude to You, O One Who Makes Mensa Look Like A Bunch Of Numbskulls By Comparison, for finding a job for their son, Frank. As this family's witnessed time and again, Frank here can be a challenge, what with his cruel streak, his fits of rage, his trips in and out of various state-run institutions, and frequent refusals to take his many medications. But You, in Your boundless wisdom, Celestial Ward Cleaver, have provided Frank with a real opportunity to utilize his unique gifts by shepherding him to his new position as Director of Veal for the ConAgra Corporation.

Again this year, as has been their custom in recent times, the young people who have gathered around the table today would like to raise a "Hosanna" to You, for continuing to forestall any kind of return to popularity by the singer Ricky Martin.

Please receive our gratitude, Thou Most Wrathful Wreaker of Wretribution, for vanquishing the unholy opponents of and quelling the profane objections to Mel Gibson's *The Passion of the Christ*. I remain hopeful that this moving, eloquent film will mark the beginning of a truly Christian cinema—a cinema of love, devotion, and righteousness that, it goes without saying, You will not allow Jewish studio executives to profit from. And whilst on the subject of entertainment, might I add that everyone in this You-fearing family would enthusiastically rejoice should You decide to grace our television with an equally pious presentation, a regularly scheduled, network program fully faithful to Your Holy Word. Maybe an hour dramedy. With Angela Lansbury. And, we humbly beseech Thee, with no subtitles.

We are furthermore eternally indebted to You for Your strength and guidance in our church's victory to have creationism added to the local public school system's science curriculum. We are confident that You will also be by our side in the upcoming year as we take up the fight to require all Math classes in the state to teach Reverend Clark's theory of the four-sided triangle.

Finally, O Jehovah, Creator of Life, Ender of Life and Chief Administrator of Comas, we thank Thee for this great country we live in. For America. For a land where women have struck Your intended perfect balance between concealing their physical beauty beneath the purdah of Islam and Hindu and parading around in the shameless nakedness of idolatrous, pagan peoples. For a country where, reasonably, democracy is adored yet, happily, voting can be ignored. Verily, though, we raise our voices in praise most high because if not for America, we'd all be stuck watching soccer or bicycle racing or fencing or some other sissy piece of crap sport on television after today's dinner.

Deliver the Lions by four and a half. We ask it in Thy name. Amen.

32 } Disarmed to the Teeth

CONFIDENTIAL MEMO

To: All local NRA chapters
From: NRA National Headquarters
Subject: School violence spin control

Fellow gun enthusiasts,

The series of fatal shootings that
have plagued America's schools over
the past decade is, of course, a serious matter (though there's a good one
going around the office about a
teacher telling her biology class
there's going to be a pop quiz and a
kid pulls a Glock from his backpack
and asks, "Who do we have to pop?").
And no one takes gun violence more
seriously than we here at the NRA.
Seriously.

Unfortunately, whenever one of these
tragic events occurs an even more
tragic event follows: gun backlash.

You've seen it. Too many times.
It's when the bleeding hearts (just
figuratively bleeding, so far) and
the antigun zealots and the namby-
pamby liberal Hollywood-ocracy don
their berets, take to the streets,
and start beating their gun control
bongo drums more vigorously, more
frequently, than I was beaten in the
slave galley of Ben-Hur. It's when
every weak-kneed Nancy and Monday-
morning peacenik between Boston and
Cambridge is shaking his or her
pathetic, empty, attached-at-the-
limp-wrist fist and holding a press
conference, giving an interview,
testifying before Congress, lobbying
local and state governments, etc.
All with the sole intent of limiting
your and my Second Amendment right
to bear insuperable weaponry (I'm
paraphrasing).

We at National Headquarters find
this assault on our core beliefs in-
tolerable. So, in an effort to fight fire
with firepower, we, along with our
public relations consultants, Barry

Emmall & Associates, have devised a
counteroffensive. One we'll need you,
the local chapters, to implement at
a grass roots level.

This counteroffensive consists of
several talking points (below), which
you should be prepared to immediately
disseminate to your area media outlets, government officials, school
boards, and, ultimately, credulous
citizens. These talking points offer
tangible, real-world solutions for
ending violence in our schools and
will, therefore, tacitly shift responsibility away from guns and gun
access, placing it instead where it
really belongs, i.e., anywhere else.

Since students, parents, and educators all influence behavior, attitudes,
and outcomes in different ways, you'll
notice we've reflected that trichotomy
by suggesting specific courses of
action for each group.

So, just as you'd only use an elephant grenade launcher to hunt ele-
phants, try to tailor your remarks
to the group you're trying to reach/
influence.

Students

* Try not to be popular or participate in sports. It's snotty
show-offs like jocks,cheerleaders,
class presidents, homecoming
queens, et al, who draw the most
fire from the bottom-dwelling type
of student who's likely to go on
a bloody rampage.

* Befriend a loser or loner. You
know who they are. Quiet, ostra-
cized, possibly bookish or really
into the Internet and/or Goth
scenes, maybe with some physical
anomaly. Start hanging with her/
him now and s/he may not pull the
trigger on you later.

* Don't make eye contact with anyone.
Especially if the other person is
looking at you through a telescopic
sight. FBI profilers report a 78
percent greater likelihood of
getting shot when eyes meet "in
the 'scope."

* Skip school as often as possible.
  It only makes sense that if you're
  not in school 50 percent of the
  time, your chances of being shot
  also drop 50 percent.

* Opt for camouflage fashions and
  clothing. Choose items that will
  blend in with the bland institutional
  decor of your particular school.
  After all, the shooter can't hit
  what he can't see. Or, if bland
  just isn't your "bag," check out
  what Tommy Hilfiger and Abercrombie
  & Fitch are doing with fashionable,
  bold-print Kevlar.

* For anyone who feels that they
  have the potential to become a
  school shooter, get in the habit
  of carrying a gun no bigger than
  a .32 caliber. That way, if you
  should draw and fire, victims
  stand a good chance of surviving
  their wounds, a mark in your favor
  come criminal sentencing time.

<u>Parents</u>
* Don't raise a zero, geek, or
  squirrel.

* Closely monitor your child's
  appearance. If the 1960s taught us
  anything it's that a weird-<u>looking</u>
  kid is more likely to be a weird-
  <u>acting</u> kid. Eliminate all tie-dye,
  bell-bottoms, platform shoes, and
  "retro" hairstyles.

* Watch for signs of despair,
  depression, violence, or antisocial
  behavior in your child and then
  quickly try to find a pill that
  will fix his/her behavior.

* Lock up all your guns or, if
  you have too many for that to
  be practical, lock up all your
  children.

* Bring lots of pets into the home.
  Countless students are alive today
  because their classmates had the
  opportunity to vent their deadly
  emotions on small, helpless
  nonhumans outside the school.

* If you yourself are arrested or convicted of a killing spree or other gun violence in the workplace, discuss your motivations and legal defense openly and honestly with your children at home.

Educators
* Encourage responsible gun handling by students by making a shooting class part of the required curriculum. The NRA is ready and willing to help schools build firing ranges and establish gun loan programs.

* No one wants kids to do drugs, but let's face it, they're going to anyway so you may as well use this to everyone's advantage. Institute a program to subtly guide students toward the drugs most likely to induce lethargy and apathy, like pot and Quaaludes, and away from drugs linked to heightened activity and excitability, like methamphetamine and crack.

* Pass "concealed carry" rules for
your school. More and more states
are recognizing that an armed
citizenry is a safer citizenry and
so should you. Think about it:
If everyone knows that a large
percentage of your student body
is always carrying a gun, how
likely is it that an angry or
despondent individual student
will draw on his/her classmates?

* Promote an atmosphere of promiscuity
and free love. Because if you can
get your entire male student body
laid, you eliminate the powerful
"hormonal factor" which tends to
prod pent-up rage into a murderous
impulse.

* Discontinue all Phys Ed activities
that work and strengthen children's
arms and upper bodies. By allowing
their musculature to atrophy,
students will soon become unable
to lift and carry bigger, heavier
weapons, like shotguns, automatic

assault rifles, even some long
barrel, large caliber handguns.
Additionally, calcium-rich, bone-
building products like milk and
cheese, as well as other high-pro-
tein foods, should be eliminated
from cafeteria menus.

I personally want to thank you in
advance for all your help on this
important issue. And let's all try to
remember: There's room for the Second
Amendment in secondary education.

Sincerely,
Charlton Heston
President, National Rifle Association

33} The Accumulation of the Wisdom of Accumulation

My fellow Americans, Walmart. Always low prices. Always.

I address the nation tonight regarding an issue of the utmost importance. An issue which, unless resolved, threatens to remain unresolved.

Since becoming president, one of my recurring top priorities has been to strengthen and revitalize the nation's economy, that is, to restore robust growth and, in the process, create jobs for the country's unworking and overunemployed. In pursuit of this objective, my administration has followed a single guiding principle: Take a two-pronged approach. Prong One has been to boldly rejigger the relationship between tax revenue and government spending; Prong B has been the establishment of a more favorable atmosphere for big business, where restrictive *laissez faire*—a timid policy rooted in the tradition of Gallic gutlessness—is replaced by lucrative *carte blanche*—a bold course of business that's 100 percent American.

For that single dual reason, I have, over the course of my term, proposed—and Congress has passed—several key pieces of legislation intended to stimulate the economy and hasten our nation's recovery. Unquestionably, those stimuluses have made a significant difference.

Do you Yahoo?

For instance, the tax cut package I signed into law in June of 2001—and, if I remember correctly, some other stuff I was told to sign in 2002, -3 and -4—put money back in the pockets of all Americans. Even those with the lowest incomes—deadbeats and whiners, people who are barely trying—received a $300 refund which they were then free to turn around and reinvest in our businesses and the economy in whatever manner they desired, whether it be a poor single parent finally taking her sick child to the doctor, an elderly couple on a fixed income setting winter thermostats up from a chilly sixty-five degrees to a more comfortable sixty-six, or a suburban soccer mom buying half a pair of Ferragamo shoes.

More importantly, the cuts eased considerably the tax burden on the wealthiest Americans—the titans of industry who generously employ and put up with the piteous multitudes; the distinguished descendents of the capitalists and industrialists who built this country; the superstar celebrities who make life worth living; in sum, the courageous top 5 percent of individuals who have tirelessy, thanklessly, assumed the awesome burden of holding and controlling 98 percent of this country's wealth. This single, simple provision had the effect of collectively incentivizing America's middle class to work harder for success, so that they might achieve the same tax advantages. As an added benefit, refunds of tens of thousands of dollars to this country's most successful, prosperous citizens—citizens recognized and accepted as role models and opinion leaders—put them in a happier, better-than-normal mood, a mood calculated to progressively trickle down to the trickle-reaping, trickle-deserving members of society. In short, those of us who have the most are happier than ever before, and those of you who don't are happier for us.

Another way we've been able to move the economy forward are the wars we successfully waged and continue to successfully

diency has created in the medical field, with increased revenues reported by myriad healthcare providers, from allergists and dermatologists to oncologists and autopsyists.

All these measures, along with others too numerous to remember, have put America back on course. And there is no doubt in my mind that today's America is headed away from the bad little part of the past and into the big good part of the future.

Visa. It's everywhere you want to be.

But for all the progress that's been made, there's more to be done. Business overall remains cautious, with few taking advantage of the Federal Reserve's continuing low interest rates. Domestic job growth is hindered by the increased use of cheap overseas labor by American companies, which, as you know, is necessitated by the noble commitment of these enterprises to make the most profit for their investors.

Given the smart, capable executives who run large corporations in this country—people I know, people Vice President Cheney knows—we all must respect their prudence and trust they're doing what's good for themselves. Because, really, we can ask no more; like it says in the Bible, "What's good for business is good for America." I can only reassure these fine businessmen and that one woman, the one who runs Hewlett Packard, that this administration will never, under any circumstances, burden any Fortune 500 company with unacceptable policies, unwanted interference, or an unlikable tax rate.

Yet, as I've indicated, a dynamic, expanding economy is absolutely essential to the security and well-being of this nation, its people, and this presidency. And let me assure you, that everyone around me seems confident this outcome can be achieved. But to do so will require the commitment of all our citizens. It will require determination. It will require blind faith, acquiescence, and obedience. Mostly, however, it will require every American to do what you do best. That is, shop, shop, shop till you drop.

Let me clarify: This administration proposes to heighten, harness, and exploit the single most consistent and persistent force among all economic indicators—consumer spending. *Your* spending. Think about it: As a nation, we have repeatedly witnessed this force defy market downturns, corporate collapses and earnings shortfalls, dotcom shakeouts, even Henny Penny-esque investment pundits, and logic itself. And while, yes, there was a post-9/11 spending slowdown, we did not let the terrorists win and soon resumed our positions behind America's shopping carts and defiantly declared, "Let's roll."

Clearly, my fellow Americans, it has been this kind of exuberant, almost irrational consumption of goods and services in the face of recession, joblessness, even war, that has long prevented a bad situation from getting worse. Only by virtue of your rampant consumerism, your ever-expanding definition of "need," your appetite for accumulation, your full embrace of a life full of stuff, has our economic soap bubble never fully burst. And for that, on behalf of you, the American people, I thank you.

Now, though, we must be prepared to take this materialism one step further: to patriotism. It's time for us all to buy more, far more. To go beyond spending what you believe to be an *optimum* amount of your incomes and spend, at minimum, a *maximum* amount. To follow the lead of the Federal government and embrace tremendous debt and deficits as merely the cost of doing business. By doing so, by becoming a more conspicuous and consummate American consumer, you'll serve as the inexhaustible fuel of the world's first economic perpetual-motion machine. A machine whereby the more individuals spend, the more American business—and America—prospers, with the result being more money making its way back to individuals via increased wages and return on financial investments. It's almost hard to believe someone smart didn't think of this before.

Building this invincible machine is within our grasp. My economic advisors assure me that if every household throughout this great land would only increase their spending by 50–60 percent, there would be a dramatic and nearly instantaneous increase in jobs, with an attendant decrease in unemployment; manufacturing plants would operate at full capacity; corporate profits would rise allowing the government to maintain steady revenue while cutting corporate tax rates; and, as a direct result, the economy would grow at a robust double-digit pace.

UPS. What can brown do for you?

As I stated earlier, a thriving economy is critical for the security of this nation. It is only with a healthy economy that we can afford to remain a superpower, be it in military might, in foreign trade arm-twistery, or in the total domination of the *Forbes* Richest People List. So it's imperative that consumer spending levels and habits be precisely defined, standardized, and systemisized.

Which brings me to the central issue I wish to address tonight.

Obviously, an economic program of such magnitude and ambition will need to be managed vigilantly, steadfastly. That's why I'm calling on Congress to create a new Department of

Personal Inventory Growth (DPIG), along with the Cabinet-level position of Director of Immoderation. The overall mission of this department shall be to set, regulate, and enforce minimum standards of consumer spending and, in this way, create a better life for all Americans. In the short term, this "better life" will be accomplished through the possession of copious goods—in the long term through economic strength, job security, and the possession of even more copious goods.

Get your best deal of the year during your local Ford Dealer's Year End Sale-A-Bration. (Heh-heh, "Sale"-a-bration. I get it. That's cute.)

The Department of Personal Inventory Growth will have broad, sweeping powers and will unite under one roof and one director scores of existing government bureaus, agencies, and commissions previously attached to other executive departments, including but not limited to, Defense, Transportation, Energy, Education, Health and Human Services, and, most especially, Commerce and Treasury. Additionally, DPIG will establish and oversee new, supplemental administrative support and service units. Units such as:

The Joint Chief Executive Officers. The Joint Chiefs will consist of ten of this country's most successful and recognizable business leaders, drawn from industries most vital to this nation's economic strength: Automotive, Oil, Technology, Pharmaceuticals, Retail, and so on. Not only will this body serve as a Virtual Board of Directors for expanding growth, increasing revenues, and opening and owning foreign markets, it will also direct and command certain intelligence and counterintelligence operations, along with a highly skilled, fully armed military force. By utilizing these resources to their fullest, foreign competitors and other threats to the American economy will be swiftly recognized and preemptively destroyed. Because sometimes the only way to level the global playing field is by blasting a few bomb craters in it.

A case in point: Recent intelligence from a variety of sources, including corporate spies, satellite surveillance, and *Motor Trend* magazine's What's New issue, indicates a Japanese carmaker is preparing to start production of a line of automobiles to be fueled by a renewable energy source, vehicles that will cost far less than American cars, and, because they're Japanese, will be far more reliable than any car made by the Big Three. Obviously, this development seriously jeopardizes our automotive industry, threatening some of this country's highest-salaried positions in the process; our beloved oil industry would also suffer; so, too, would any business who's revenue growth depends on the ozone's continued depletion and the accompanying global warming, companies like Coppertone and other makers of high SPF suntan lotions, Speedo swimwear, Teva sandals, and so on. The Japanese cannot be permitted to make such an automotive assault on our homeland or our homeasphalt. And I can tell you they won't. Because I've personally spoken to the men I intend to name as Joint CEOs, and they've unanimously assured me they'll act in the best interests of the United States and, as their first order of business, launch a military strike on the plants turning out these Autos of Mass Destruction, reducing them to rubble and thus eliminating an imminent economic threat before a single American life, or lifestyle, is lost.

Coming to theaters this summer, Jim Carrey is *The Six Million Dollar Man.*

Another important body within the Department of Personal Inventory Growth will be the Commission on Upgrades,

Updates, and Redecoration. It will be their responsibility to institute strict guidelines and timetables by which we will all acquire and replace the various products and commodities in our lives.

For instance, I intend to ask the Committee to make it mandatory for every American household to upgrade their high tech equipment—computers, cell phones, televisions, MP3 players, anything with a microprocessor—within six months of a major advance in chip technology. Furthermore, in categories as diverse as footwear and furniture, cars to cartoon character-licensed merchandise, color, taste, and fashion cycles will, by law, be shortened drastically, thus forcing trendsetters and trendslaves alike to restock and revamp their lives at a faster, more profitable pace than the current fourteen-month norm. I will also recommend the following measures to the Commission: That homeowners, through either the purchase of a new home or room addition, must increase their living space by 1,500 square feet every five years; that durable goods be phased out in favor of less durable goods; and that failure to keep up with the Joneses be made a felony offense.

DPIG's Federal Bureau of Ingestion will make this country's obesity epidemic a priority. Specifically, they'll be trying to speed the expansion of the American waistline through increased food purchase and consumption. Economic impact studies show that the increased healthcare costs associated with obesity can be more than offset by revenues generated by putting the country on a four-meal-a-day regimen and strict enforcement of new laws governing constant snacking. Not only because restaurants, grocery stores, farmers, and related businesses will benefit from improved food sales, but because once our obesity rate ticks up to 50 percent, 60 percent, 70 percent, the whole country—the whole world—will have to be rebuilt, restructured, reinforced, to accommodate our more massive physiques.

Imagine for a moment the economic windfall of widening every interior and exterior door from sea to shining sea. Of replacing the narrow, inadequate chairs in each home, office, and public space. Of rebuttressing all our floors, balconies, and decks. Of converting military cargo jets to passenger jets. Of an electric scooter in every garage and under every ever-spreading backside. These and countless other modifications and adaptations strongly suggest obesity is a big, fat, revenue-generating dream come true. A way to turn lemons into lemonade with extra sugar and two dips of lemon sherbet served with a slice of lemon pie with a cookie crust. And I pledge to you, the Federal Bureau of Ingestion shall be the unambiguous link which binds our rounder individual silhouettes to a sounder shared economy, the instrument that will forever change our view of the obese from "American hippo" to "American hero."

McDonald's. I'm lovin' it. Tell 'em, "The Prez sent me" and when you buy two McGriddles you'll get a third free.

Of course, transforming unrestrained consumption from a national priority to a national obsession can't be accomplished through a mere act of government. It must also be an act of personal will. So, through the formation of the Commercial and Advertising Communication Agency (CACA) we'll help create and drive that will.

The Agency's top priority will be to keep consumer demand at peak levels, 24/7/360-whatever, to stoke the fires of desire through the total ubiquitization of advertising messages. In other words, CACA shall seek to make all public and private horizontal and vertical surfaces, all public speech and events, all publications, films, and art, as well as broadcast and narrowcast media, carriers of commercial messages.

The changes the Agency will oversee will be many. No longer will the wearing of non-logo'd—non-*working*, non-*productive*—T-shirts or ball caps be socially acceptable or, under Federal law, permissible. Also, product image-enhancing sponsorships will no longer be restricted to the grandest events or places, such as the Tostitos Fiesta Bowl or Qual-Comm Stadium; instead, CACA will broker endorsements across the size spectrum, like Olympic Water Seal's Your Son's Treehouse and The Northwestern Mutual Funeral of Ed Thompson. Hollywood will be called upon to do its part, too, by taking product placement to the next level, producing films along the lines of *Finding Nemo with the Raytheon L750 Fish Finder eAngler, The Steinway Pianist,* and *Indiana Jones and the Office of Indiana Travel and Tourism.* And by 2006, a sophisticated nationwide network of lasers will beam brand logos onto all the clouds in the sky.

As some of you have undoubtedly noticed, I, your nominal president, am already doing my part, interspersing commercial messages throughout my address. Needless to say, the purpose here, first and foremost, is to increase awareness of some fine brands. But these messages are also paid messages, with the income generated tonight covering lawn service at the White House for a full year. Let me add, too, in the spirit of bipartisanship and co-promotion, the Democratic response to my address tonight will be sponsored in its entirety by Dodge Ram Trucks, who invite you to grab life by the horns.

Get rid of stubborn athlete's foot with tough actin' Tinactin.

Though managing and coordinating the aforementioned agencies will undoubtedly be a formidable task, that is just a small part of what my Director of Immoderation will be called on to perform.

One of my first directives to the Director will be to search out unprecedented, unexplored avenues of purchase and replacement, such as investigating how we might require those over the age of twenty-one who have lost a parent or parents to purchase new ones. Or creating a new kind of surgery, a surgery that's not really emergency and not quite elective, but more like "imposed."

Nexium. Relieve the heartburn. Heal the damage.

I believe another of the nation's biggest opportunities for increased consumption flows from our smallest citizens, if you don't count midgets and dwarves. I speak, of course, of our children.

Now, many, many parents are already lavishing their babies, toddlers, adolescents, and teens with an improbable number of toys, electronics, lessons, clothing, entertainments, and comestibles. But pockets of parental restraint remain *and this cannot stand.* America can no longer afford to teach its children the concepts of sufficiency or contentment or give love, support, and so-called "quality time" in place of tangible goods. In other words, the time for Universal Child Spoilage (UCS) is here.

To make certain this goal is achieved, the Director of Immoderation will explore the most efficapacious way to implement UCS. Until that exploration is complete, I expect him to use the bully pulpit of his office to persuade every adult—from parents and grandparents to aunts, uncles, and, yes, even Santa—that, when it comes to acquiescing to a child's demands for toys and candy, the moon and the stars, less is *not only* not more, more is *less than enough.* And believe me, neither The Department of Personal Inventory Growth nor this administration will consider our jobs finished until all children, from the daughter of the lowest lower-middle class family to the son of a president, get everything their hearts desire, everything money can buy, and everything the traffic will allow.

Playstation. Live in your world. Play in ours.

Finally, I'd like to say a few words to those Americans who may be wondering how they'll be able to make and afford these abundant purchases. Those few words are, "Easy credit terms. You can't be turned down."

By this I mean the newly formed Department of Personal Inventory Growth, as its first official act, will triple every American's credit limit. Instantly. Across the board. Without time-consuming, often disqualifying questions and forms. Working illegal aliens will have their credit limits doubled. Furthermore, minimum monthly payments can be extended over the lifespans of up to two future generations.

But there are those among us who may not be anxious to accept this credit increase. I'm speaking of those rare and peculiar citizens who have lived within their means, who have scrimped and saved and salted away money in a passbook or money market account. Maybe they've put this money away for a prospective college education or retirement or a just a rainy day. My fellow Americans, given this country's current economic situation, such funds will from this day forward be considered obstructive and unpatriotic; those who hold these accounts will be strongly urged to exhaust them. To facilitate the separation of these savers from their savings, banks, rather than paying interest, are hereby authorized to *charge* interest for tending and protecting a citizen's money. Meaning that to withhold one's funds from the marketplace is to see them erode from disuse.

This week's Powerball jackpot is up to $130,000,000. Remember, you can't win if you don't play.

Before I leave you tonight, I'd like to reaffirm my belief that once The Department of Personal Inventory Growth has been approved by Congress, once its agencies are formed and operative, its programs implemented, this nation's economy will flourish as never before. Your lives will be full of exponentially more goods and therefore more happiness. Worry, want, and worrisome wanting will be things of the past. Because just as The Department of Homeland Security eradicated terrorism, so, too, will The Department of Personal Inventory Growth eradicate any weakness in the economy.

My fellow Americans, to borrow a phrase from the great President Ronald Reagan's great advertising campaign, a new day is dawning in America. A fine, fair day of perpetual prosperity and periodic peace. Where "How much is that?" is never asked and "I'll take it" never stifled. Where disposable income is indistinguishable from income. Where the disproportion of your possessions in comparison to other world citizens is no longer a shameful tenfold but a self-satisfying thousandfold. Where the stock market bulls run on an endless and ever increasingly speedily spinning treadmill. And where my saying something is true, is as good as its being so.

Thank you, goodnight, and get the good night's sleep you need with Sominex.

34 } Serious Happiness

Happiness. You can find it anywhere. You may find it nowhere. Men commonly believe it can be found in a woman's underwear. Women, on the other hand, seek their happiness at a deeper, more intrinsic, elemental level, unless sidetracked by an incredible storewide shoe sale.

To be truly and thoroughly happy is to have a smile on your face, a spring in your step, a song in your heart and a maraca in your duodenum.

Happiness goes by many names: Joy. Delight. Elation. Antifrownism. Negative negativism. Sustained N_2O. The good kind of crazy. Botched indifference. Half a mood swing. John Denver's plane is missing. Grading life on the curve. Al Gore has won Florida. Cheerleaders' disorder. Laying the hangover's groundwork. All that being said, the fact is it's not really important what you call happiness so long as you remember what you've filed it under.

Happiness comes in a limitless variety of shapes and sizes, though the best shapes and sizes are frequently on backorder or held aside for wealthy, influential friends of the Happiness Distributor. Depending on who you are, happiness can be as simple as seeing your whole family gathered for a Sunday picnic or as complicated as arranging to have each and every one of them iced by a professional killer over the course of an unsuspicious stretch of time. It might be as whimsical as a boy band with the clap or as unexpected and deeply fulfilling as the phrase, "suspended sentence." But one thing we should not lose sight of is that the pursuit of happiness and the pursuit of the one-armed man can be undertaken concurrently.

Each year, we purchase cards exhorting friends and family to have a Happy New Year, a Happy St. Patrick's Day, a Happy Easter, a Happy Thanksgiving, and a Happy Birthday when, in reality, their true purpose is to make a Happy Hallmark Corporation.

Ignorance is not bliss; ignorance of Billy Joel's *oeuvre* is bliss.

Happiness is an unpredictable and capricious companion, often fleeting, at other times settled, so always keep in mind that should any change in its arrival or departure times become necessary, there will be a $75 reticketing charge. Those who are truly happy look happy, which explains the collective facial expression on any given city bus. Just because your friends can't find happiness doesn't mean you can't find happiness in the unhappiness of your friends. The opposite of happiness is not sadness, the opposite of happiness is the banter of local news teams.

To raise and reside beneath the Canopy of Happiness it is necessary to possess at least one of the Four Pillars of Joy: (1) A bartender with a heavy pour. (2) Being a member of a target demographic no advertiser wishes to reach. (3) Knowing how to count to four.

Happiness must meet a higher standard in the present day than in the past. In medieval times, a man considered it a "joyful day" if he remained unbeheaded, Black Death-free, or didn't have to go outside wearing those gay-looking tights. Pre-1851, Americans reveled in the fact that *Moby Dick* hadn't been written yet and so couldn't be assigned to them in their lit classes. But today, happiness is expected to be more frequent, more intense and more personal, hence multiple HBOs. As for our future descendants, we can only surmise that they will know the greatest of all happinesses when their giant brains are able to devise a convincing looking hairpiece to cover their giant, pulsing, bald brain heads.

To be upbeat or optimistic is to be within spitting distance of happiness. *Easy* spitting distance if you're especially phlegmy.

Happiness, regardless of its type or intensity, its brevity or longevity, is essentially spiritual. Or, if not, Oprah is a lying bitch. Some believe the ultimate happiness awaits them in the afterlife, and for those of you who have chosen the *right* religion and worshipped the *right* Supreme Being the *right* amount with the *right* holy book and supplicated yourselves on the *right* day of the week under the guidance of the *right* spiritual leaders who wear the *right* headgear and the *right* flowing robes and display the *right* icons, that's undoubtedly true; for everyone else, *your* first meeting with The Creator promises to be something more on the order of "uncomfortable." Beyond happiness is rapture, beyond rapture is when a new kid shows up in school one day and people start calling him "pizza face" instead of you.

Charles Schulz, the wise and witty creator of *Peanuts,* defined it thus: "Happiness is a warm puppy," to which I can only add, "...unless it got that way in the microwave."

35 } Stop Thinking About Doing It and Do It

Come and knock on our door. (Come and knock on our door.) We've been waiting for you. (We've been waiting for ...) Heeey. Check out Willie Loman at the newsstand there. Willie Loman? He's fictional. How's some real guy look like a fictional character? I don't know. I guess, the hunched posture. Old and tired. The sample case. Well, not a sample case, exactly. That thing looks more like a big book of carpet samples. Do carpet salesmen make house calls? Probab ... Damn, we should've looked into that before we bought our carpet. Maybe he could've told us that ours was going to show every dog hair the dog shedded. Shedded? Is that the past tense of shed? Or maybe shed is the past tense? OK, then what's the present tense? For that matter, what's the past tense of blow dry? Blown dry? Blow dried? Blew dry? Who would know that that I could ask?... Where the kisses are hers and hers and his, Three's Company, too ... Anyway, there's so much damn dog hair, what rug wouldn't show it. But that's the breed. They shed a lot. (That's it, keep it in the present.) But this seems like more shedding than usual. Maybe I should get her checked at the vet. Next week. After I get paid. Oh, man, that's not right. To wait. Just cuz I'm broke. Like always anymore. Fuck. I gotta get old Mr. Asshole to give me a raise. The jerk. I'm going nowhere there. I oughta just quit. ... Come and dance on our floor. (Come and dance on our floor.) Try a step that is new ...

Ever experience this type of thought pattern? Nonproductive. Barely interesting. Just enough anxiety to be annoying. Endlessly tangential. Perhaps with a detestable, looping sound-track. Do you ever hear a part of your brain telling the rest of your brain to shut up? Are your intracranial concoctions *far-katke?* If so, you may be one of the millions of Americans who suffer from hypercognitive discharge (HCD) or, as it's more commonly known, "mindless thinking."

If I take a little bottle of pure black atoms—carbon, maybe—and I have some way of putting them on a pure white surface one atom at a time, one right next to the other, but not in a straight line, like in a bunch, a cluster, I wonder how many atoms I have to clump together there before they're visible to the naked eye?

Mindless thinking doesn't imply an especially high or low IQ. Or madness. Or a magic mushroom addiction. And it's not telling you you're not busy enough. (True, one of the most common, recurring "mindless thoughts" people have is one that scolds the self for sitting around thinking all the time, i.e., not "doing something"; but the point we're making here is that the overall disorder, HCD itself, isn't indicative of a par-ticularly sedentary or stagnant way of life.) No, mindless thinking is indiscriminate. Random. It can afflict anyone with a brain. From a synchrotron physicist to 'N Sync. Symptoms associated with the condition include difficulty relaxing, difficulty sleeping, difficulty concentrating, difficulty listening to others, difficulty making decisions, and difficulty not get-ting highly irritated when someone repeats the same noun over and over again even though you know there are plenty of suitable synonyms and can cite three without picking up the *Roget's* or even trying very hard.

* * *

Hey, you're just here for a drink. You're allowed. If she happens to be here, so what? Just ignore her. No. Wrong. Acknowledge her. But just a nod. No, a wave. Maybe a half-nod and a half-wave. Yeah. Unless she's with somebody. Then ignore her. No, don't even let her see you. No, no, start talking to the babe on your left here, and let her see me then. See how she likes th ... wait. That works if she's with a guy. If she's here with a girlfriend, though, I'll ... Well, if she's with Heather, I'll act like everything's fine, buy them a drink, but if it's that bitch Amy, I'll just look the other way. No, because if Amy sees me she'll start trashing me, telling Shelly, "Look who's here acting like he's too good to say 'Hello'" and all kinds of shit. So maybe I preempt that with ...

Today, however, just as medical science has helped the egregiously proboscisized with rhinoplasty, the immensely bazoomed with breast reduction surgery, and the flagrantly immense with stomach staples and the Fobi pouch, there's relief for overthinkers. It's a fast, simple procedure called the Druling Pleat, developed by neurosurgeon and cranial pioneer, Dr. Yura Druling. The Druling Pleat (so-called because of the "notch, fold, and suture" technique applied to the patient's front orbital lobe) is a strategic reduction in brain mass designed to eliminate stray thoughts, shrink nagging anxieties, purge pointless rumination. And, in a majority of cases, do it without disturbing problem-solving skills, creativity, or motor functions.* You get all the upside of thinking with none of the downside. Because now, the only "chatter" you'll hear between big ideas or in the background of your daily activities is a soft, comforting, innocuous intracranial white noise (Mountain Brook, Woodland Glade, Ocean Surf, and Bobby McFarrin soundscapes available at extra charge).

* * *

I want a fifth bowl of ice cream .... *It's nice that the salesman wants me to meet the dealership's sales manager* .... *I'm in the middle of dinner ... The phone is ringing ... I better get it* .... *Time to host my radio talk show* ....

Best of all, once you have the Druling Pleat, you'll never think about it again. No regrets. No doubts. No concerns. And isn't that the point? To let science take care of your problem, then get on with the rest of our life?

The Druling Pleat. Today's easy way to zap the crap right out of your brain.

---

*Side effects associated with the Druling Pleat include: mouth-breathing; bowling; a subscription to *People* magazine; mistaking the ottoman for your dog and your dog for Orchan, first sultan of the Ottoman Empire; increased bus ridership; the acceptance of Jesus Alou as your personal savior; sudden urges to pass concealed weapon legislation; wearing loafers with no socks; and a radically diminished grasp of what constitutes medical malpractice.

36 } Monkey See, Monkey Will Take a Pass

The chip that powers my aging PC is to the chips that power the latest PCs, as the rhesus money is to the bulbous-headed giant brain people of the 51st Century. My computer's motherboard is a candidate for a hysterectomy. The operating system pre-dates DOS; rather it is UNO. Expressed in miles, my hard drive is googols from giga. I possess so little RAM I'm technically a EWE with a hormone imbalance. My keyboard is not wireless. My lap is laptopless. My only Palm device is a joy buzzer (non-programmable).

I own a machine that *plays* CDs but not one that *burns* CDs. My video system is TV and VCR, not HDTV and DVD. My picture tube would be considered "big screen" only by someone willing to watch it with his or her nose pressed up against the glass. I waste my evenings staring mindlessly at a single broadcast channel, not churning endlessly through 200 cable channels. My sound does not so much surround as snipe. I take photos with film rather than pixels. My idea of a 128-bit video game system is trying to maneuver the little steel balls into the kitty's eyes after smoking a joint. I cannot be paged. I cannot be beeped. I do not know how to page or beep others. I'm completely unclear as to how the pageable and beepable are related to the moveable and shakeable. My phones all have cords.

I do not live in a Glen, Knoll, Valley, Trace, or Meadow. I do not reside on a Ridge, Point, or Green. Size-wise, my home would appear to be the aborted fetus of the homes that constitute most Glens, Knolls, Valleys, Traces, Meadows, Ridges, Points, and Greens. Inside my house, you'll find no media room, no master suite, no breakfast room, bonus room or first-floor laundry room, no cathedral ceilings, no restaurant-quality appliances, no decorator touches. My furnishings are more motley than Mia Farrow's children. There is no hot tub, whirlpool, sauna or steam room, meaning that in order to satisfy the primal human need to be hot, wet, and naked simultaneously I have to rub Ben-Gay all over my body and run through the sprinkler. My house has but one bathroom; my bathroom has but one sink; my sink has but one of whatever it's supposed to have two of. My garage is one car.

I do not have my own Web page. Or home page. Or Web site. Or home Web. Or page site. Or wome sige. My domain is unnamed, unregistered, unclear, and undefended. The only server I have ever relied on is Ruth, the sweet, old gal down at the Toddle House who always remembers to bring me ketchup with my scrambled eggs and calls me "Hon." I find dot coms intriguing only insofar as I can't figure out why they aren't called "period coms." I have not blogged since second grade when I accidentally blogged my pants at recess. I have never shopped an "e-tailer." I have never bid in an "e-auction." I don't know how to "e-trade." I have never perused an "e-book." I do on occasion say, "Eeeee-doggies." Activities done in "real time" sound to me like the antithesis of a "real good time."

My car goes from 0–60 in a time span entirely unworthy of measure or mention. Its engineering would be considered a

37 } Split Focus

The Master of the Action Allegory. The "limited-theatrical-release"-filmmaker's filmmaker. The intellectual's Hal Needham. The moron's Akira Kurosawa.

Only one director could inspire such an impressive array of sobriquets: Jacques Auph, the highly low- profile, overly underutilized *auteur*. The nicknames derive from his style of moviemaking, which film scholars have classified as "introspective commercialism," that is, a fusion of the personal, expressive, even symbolic, highbrow art film and the special-effects-laden, testosteronic global blockbuster. Auph, a slow and deliberate craftsman who has made a total of ten feature films over his thirty-five year (so far) career, is not only the form's originator, he is its sole practitioner. "I've always lived by my own rules," he says. "My own traffic code and zoning restrictions, too."

Auph comes by his artistic bipolarity naturally. His parents are French New Wave director Marc Auph and actress Yvette Monsfelt, the blonde, buxom star of *Attack of the Sizable Ants, Double Date with the Devil, Podiatry College Confidential* and dozens of other Hollywood B-movies in the 1950s and 1960s. "Perhaps, subconsciously, I'm trying to please them both," Auph said in a recent interview, "but on a conscious level, I'm glad they're both dead."

Unfortunately, for both the filmmaker and the film-going public, Auph's work has not been widely distributed or shown.

("Rob Schneider movies typically open on more screens than mine," states the director, who, like the rest of America, curses the day Rob Schneider was born.) But it would seem Auph's obscurity is about to come to an end. Next month, cinephiles will be able to view much of this modern master's *oeuvre* when Manhattan's avant-garde Museum of What We're Calling Art This Week begins a major retrospective called "Hollywouldn't." The show consists of eight films screened over eight weeks. (Noticeably absent from the program are two pictures many consider Auph's best: *Scenes from an Intergalactic Mating Ritual* and *Claire's Knee Is Missing!* Asked why, museum curator Lily Whitenrich explains, "Explanations are meaningless." Then adds, "But don't look at me."). Scheduled to be presented are:

The Seventh Cereal Grain (1978): Plotnik (John Cassavetes) is a desperate man dying of colon cancer. His last hope is an experimental treatment that would have a micro-miniaturized vessel and crew (including Jon Voight and Adrienne Barbeau) carrying a high-fiber remedy—the "Seventh Cereal Grain" of the title—injected directly into his lower large intestine. Auph treats audiences to spectacular special effects inside the body as the crew fights its way to the "drop zone" (the duodenum), battling "huge" bacteria, parasites, and other organisms along the way. The "outside" story of Plotnik's struggle with the Hegelian concept of death, however, makes this film just as emotionally moving as it is bowel moving. Thought to be the first film to depict someone playing Parcheesi with the allegorical figure of Dietary Fiber as represented by the Quaker Oats Quaker.

Marzipan Badge (1981): Candy is often associated with children and innocence, but here Auph uses sweets as a symbolic counterpoint to the bitterness that's accumulated within a failed relationship. Marta (Faye Dunaway) is a confectioner whose marriage to Olm (Max von Sydow), the Stockholm Police Commissioner, is crumbling. Life worsens when the press breaks a police corruption story and Olm, though innocent, is made the scapegoat. Now, out of office and forbidden to carry or purchase a weapon, Olm must somehow figure a way to restore his reputation. But gunless he's no match for the heavily armed evildoers behind his fall. Enter Marta. Working smoothly side-by-side, the couple creates licorice whip garrotes, peanut brittle daggers, candy cane nunchucks, gummy bludgeons, a whole arsenal of "sweet destruction," which Olm uses to savage his foes and reclaim his good name. Auph's final shot—Marta and Olm, back in the candy kitchen, literally bound together by sticky, spilled nougat, yet struggling to break free—is a masterpiece of ambiguity.

The Lamborghini Thief (1984): Leo, an impoverished, out-of-work laborer (Dennis Hopper), steals an Italian sports car in order to drive to the store and get a loaf of day-old bread for his young son, Sal (Ricky Schroeder). On the way to the market, however, he shifts into fourth gear and—*mirabile dictum*—discovers the car is a time machine and winds up driving a week into the future. Once there, though, he is devastated to discover that, because he never got to the market, he did not get the bread and, as a result, he and his son have starved to death. Raging against cruel fate, Leo returns to his own time and goes on a killing spree, knowing that if he's caught, he won't serve much time in prison because he's already seen that he's going to be dead in a week anyway. A powerful statement on the politics of poverty, the nature of time, and the extraordinary father/son bond that only blood vengeance can forge.

8.5 Seconds (1988): An action film about action filmmaking. For the climax of his latest motion picture, Director Speed Labateau (played by Auph himself) is attempting to create the most exciting, explosive, fast-paced, thrill-packed, dangerous, and heart-stopping 8.5-second film sequence in cinematic history. We're with Labateau the entire way as he madly dashes from digital effects lab to green screen to robotic modeling facility at an Industrial Light and Magic-like compound locked in a frantic race against the clock, only to come in thirty-six days late and $43 million over budget.

Ty Cobb: The Wrath of God (1991): A brooding, profound biopic of the mean-spirited, obnoxious Hall of Famer (played with silent intensity by Joe Pesci). This picture has been both hailed and reviled for its highly symbolic final sequence in which Cobb decapitates Casey Stengel (James Woods) and finds the skull full of peanuts and Crackerjack. Entire film is told from the baseball bat's point of view (voice of Michael J. Fox).

Il Postino Ballistico (1993): Set in New York's Little Italy, this film traces the life of Gianni Carbinierri (Robert De Niro), an overworked postal worker who develops an unlikely friendship with Cary Abaggadeau (Michael Douglas), a wealthy homeowner residing on his delivery route. Over time, Gianni comes to find out that Abaggadeau heads the largest direct mail advertising agency—i.e., junk mailer,—in America and is therefore largely responsible for his (Gianni's) crushing work-load. This perceived betrayal of their friendship, pushes the stressed mail carrier to his emotional threshold...and a gun shop. In a torrent of violence and mayhem, Gianni (and Auph) shows us the emptiness of dreams, the desolation of man's soul, and the beauty of 10,000 squibs and a tanker truck of movie blood. Naming *Il Postino Ballistico* to his Ten Best List of 1994, Roger Ebert wrote, "...so beautiful you'll weep blood."

Paleozoic Sanctuary (1998): On a remote, South Sea island, sci-entists (Anthony Hopkins, Tim Robbins and Holly Hunter) regenerate extinct species of prehistoric flora. Soon, how-ever, the plants threaten to overgrow and entangle the vari-ous buildings and their inhabitants. Fortunately, even the most fecund vegetation only grows a couple of inches a day and the scientists have brought plenty of pruners so disaster is calmly averted. Less about man's meddlesome ways and special effects than a thoughtful, even-handed rumination on compost.

Gray Matters (2001): It is 1995 and, through a combination of droll coincidence and medical hubris, the brains of murder-ous West African despot President Idi Ghormai (Samuel L. Jackson) and IRA bomber Shamus Fershore (Daniel Day-Lewis) are switched in a London hospital. The result is two men struggling to retain their identities and respective desires to kill large numbers of a specific population even as they struggle to regain control of their bodily motor functions. Through this construct, Auph is able to juxtapose black and white, oppressor and oppressed, exploding First Worlders and machete'd Third Worlders, drooling and incontinence, to ironic effect and thereby demonstrate that it is not absolutes but, as the title suggests, shades of gray that dominate our existence. The denouement of native-garbed Africans marching drunk in Belfast's St. Patrick's' Day Parade is often hailed as, "What the…?"

The director will participate in a brief question-and-answer session in the museum auditorium after each Thursday's final showing, though the audience will be asked to leave before he questions and answers himself.

38 } Stage Frightening

As one might guess, the little town where I spend most of my year, Death to Shakespeare, New Mexico, is not a hotbed of theater. This is too bad. Because I love a good play or musical. So, rather than make do with the local elementary school's production of *The Gin Game*, I make it a point to go to New York City as often as I can. There, I'm able to thoroughly indulge my theater bug, until it's stretched and swollen like an engorged tick.

Of course, the next best thing to seeing a play is sharing it with others. Here's a brief account of the shows I saw during my most recent stay in New York:

Oaklahomies: A big, bold, hip-hop "revival/reworking" of the classic musical, *Oklahoma*. In this version—set in the inner city of present day Oakland, California—a fly honey is gamed by both a phat banger and a def gangsta. Then things get wack. Just the way Rogers & Hammerstein wrote it, just the way you remember it! Songs include: "Oh, What a Beautiful Motherfuckin' Mornin'," and "The Brutha With the 'Fro on the Top."

I Come When I Call: An absorbing Absurdist drama by Skru Ue, a Balinese playwright, who, as a young man, maintained close contact with his idol Samuel Beckett (through hundreds of prank phone calls) and was later employed by Harold Pinter to cut the crusts off his sandwiches. The play opens on a darkened stage. A soft, single spotlight illuminates an unidentified man, sitting, alone, making explicit phone sex calls. By the end of the first act, the man has discovered he's so dependent on and fulfilled by these calls that he's fallen in love with the telephone. He then marries the phone and they settle down in the suburbs of Grand Forks, North Dakota. But, as the second act reveals, they do not live happily ever after. Because the man is white and the phone is black, the couple is shunned by their narrow-minded, intolerant neighbors. In the final scene, desperate and dispirited, he and his touch-tone bride call Information and inquire as to the meaning of life, at which point they are told this can only be revealed if they're willing to switch to Sprint as their long distance carrier.

Chernobyl, Chernobyl: The spectacular, bright, flashy new musical based on the Soviet nuclear accident and its aftermath. Produced and directed by Julie Taymor, the creative force behind (most famously) Disney's *The Lion King.* In her greatest stroke of stagecraft yet, Taymor has actually irradiated and mutated cast members for an ultra-realistic-yet-surrealistic flavor. Don't miss this one.

What's That You're Eating, Nikola?: This true, fascinating drama focuses on Serbian genius Nikola Tesla (1856–1943) and recounts how he nearly went mad struggling against the accepted limits of pastry only to invent the Croissandwich.

The Mighty Quinn: Having "adapted for the stage" Bible stories (for *Joseph and the Amazing Technicolor Dreamcoat* and *Jesus Christ Superstar),* a book of poems (for *Cats)* and two movies *(Phantom of the Opera* and *Sunset Boulevard),* Sir Andrew Lloyd

Webber now draws on a whole new medium: American television. In this lavishly staged musical, the composer brings together Cannon, Barnaby Jones, Richard Kimble *(The Fugitive)*, Inspector Lewis Erskine *(The F.B.I.)*, and other lead characters from various Quinn Martin-produced hour dramas of the 1960s and 1970s. Each protagonist is still quick with a right cross and ferreting out the bad guys, but now they're even quicker with a song. Lyrics are actual dialogue from the original television scripts, all set to Webber's immensely popular "blandiose" melodies. When this was first staged in London last fall, The Guardian gushed, "Sir Andrew has successfully taken the 'tube' out of 'boob tube.'"

Boing: Stomp with springs.

How Much Would You Expect to Pay to See A Play Like This?: The mesmerizing Ron Popeil performs his scrumptious one-man show of back-to-back-to-back "info-one-acts"—*Rotisserie, Pasta Maker,* and *Food Dehydrator.* Probably the best reviewed show in recent years, *The New York Times* wrote "...imagine Willie Loman possessed with the showmanship of Nathan Lane..." The Post raved, "...makes you wonder why Spaulding Gray never made turkey jerky." The night I saw it, Mr. Popeil was called back on stage, only to further dazzle us with his timeless set piece, *Pocket Fisherman.*

First Tingle in Atlanta: Like the film it's based on, this play was originally titled *Last Tango in Paris.* The play underwent major reworking and rewriting, however, when out-of-town audiences said they thought this drama sounded too final, too musical, and too foreign.

Khmade for Each Other: A sparkling romantic comedy combining droll Coward-esque dialogue, the familial themes of *Our Town,* and the East meets West dichotomy of *The King and I.* The time is the early 1970s. Heng Ng is a Cambodian peasant farmer. Jessica Galbraeth, Ph.D., is a UN agronomist touring Southeast Asia. His parents are Khmer Rouge, hers are Princeton professors. But when Jessica falls for Heng (literally!) in a rice paddy, they soon discover love doesn't care about education. Or re-education. Too bad their clashing clans don't agree! Warm, witty, and winning.

In a Tiled Place: This unique Off-Off-Broadway comedy is, believe it or not, both high concept and lowest common denominator (or, as I read in *The New Yorker,* "vulgarious"). The play's "action" all takes place within the confines of the Stern family bathroom, where long-suffering constipation "victim" Sy Stern is perched on the toilet, lamenting his fate and warding off intruders. This is essentially a one-man show (though other unseen family members can be heard talking to Sy through the door are never actually seen on stage). Very funny and ultimately, not to spoil the ending, moving. Also features infectious catch phrases, like, "I'm tryin' to take a *crap* in here" and "Who's the friggin' wise guy that invented cheese?"

Totally Folked: A complex, human drama where love, the legal system, and science have conspired to give ten-year-old Nic Ajax four sets of parents: adoptive, biological, surrogate, and foster. Some of them are tender and nurturing, some wise and knowing, some earthy and perceptive. Too bad Nic can't always remember which are which. The third act builds to nothing less than an emotional crucible as Nic tries to get a quorum on whether he can go out and play.

Second City in a Parallel Universe: Stephen Hawking and a troupe of slightly less well-known (but highly energetic) theoretical physicists make their stage debuts in this evening of improvisational comedy sketches where punch lines are expressed as mathematical formulae.

Needless to say, by the end of my twelfth show in as many days, I was ready to return home to New Mexico. Where, I've since learned, by delaying curtain up until well past their normal bedtimes, *The Gin Game*'s little actors were cranky enough to bring their roles to delightful life.

39 } A Star is Reborn

BOB GOEN: Good evening and welcome to *Entertainment Tonight*. I'm Bob Goen....

MARY HART: ...and I'm Mary Hart. Tonight's big story is the arrival of Jesus Christ in the city of Jerusalem just over twenty-four hours ago. As you can imagine, it was absolute bedlam as the Christian Messiah made His long-awaited and triumphant "second coming" in the city that holds so many memories for Him. *ET* was there from start to finish and our own Maria Menounos kicks off our coverage. Maria, what's the lowdown?

MARIA MENOUNOS: Well, Mary, much like His first visit here just over two thousand years ago, Jesus Christ came to the holy city of Jerusalem on the back of a donkey. But unlike the original Palm Sunday, this truly charismatic Superstar was greeted and mobbed by throngs of celebrities, believers, zealots, autograph seekers, even some curious infidels. As you can see, Jesus' procession made its way slowly down the narrow, crowded streets. But the man behind Christmas maintained His legendary beatific demeanor, warmly waving to His fans the entire way. By the way, the white, full-length robe Jesus is wearing was made for Him by favorite designer Giorgio Armani and His oxen-leather sandals are from Hugo Boss.

As you'd expect, security along the route was tight, but as the Chief of Police told me....

CHIEF OF POLICE: We're watching things closely. You never know when some lunatic with a cross, hammer, and nails might jump out of the crowd.

MARIA MENOUNOS: When the Savior finally reached the end of His route, He dismounted, was quickly ushered through a wall of cameras and reporters, then whisked into the Jerusalem Crowne Plaza for His highly anticipated press conference. For that story, let's go to Mark Steines inside the hotel....

MARK STEINES: It was a very loose, very personable, completely unflappable Prince of Peace who stepped up to the microphones to take questions from the international press corps this afternoon....

CNN: How does it feel to be back in Jerusalem?

JESUS: Terrific. But I've never had a problem *entering* Jerusalem, it's the *leaving* that's proved thorny. So to speak.

MARK STEINES: He fielded questions on topics from baptism to last rites and everything in-between. And by the time He was done, He'd won the press's heart, if not its soul....

AL JAZEERA: A lot of people doubted you even existed. Anything to say to them?

JESUS: Yeah. Try not to die. [Laughter.] But if you do, dress in something very lightweight. Like a dry rub or a marinade. [Laughter and applause.]

REUTERS: You've alluded to the afterlife, and that brings up an interesting question: How can the average person get to heaven?

JESUS: Turn right at Alpha Centauri. [Laughter.]

MARK STEINES: But the most surprising exchange had to be this one...

PEOPLE: Julia Roberts has been spotted backstage at Your last two miracles. Is Your relationship serious?

JESUS: To me, Julia is one of My Father's most beautiful creations, nothing more.

MARK STEINES: The press conference lasted about thirty minutes, during which Christ was asked questions on everything from who His favorite disciple was—Simon Peter, in case you're interested—to the true nature of His relationship with the infamous Mary Magdalene. On that subject, He had only this to say....

JESUS: I did *not* have sexual relations with that woman.

MARK STEINES: Throughout the Q & A, Christ was alternately enigmatic and charismatic. But clearly, by the end of the session, he had reporters absolutely mesmerized as He recounted His brief, "unbilled," incognito return to Earth, when, because He foresaw they'd soon stop touring, He attended the Beatles' Shea Stadium concert in August, 1966. Which led to this revealing exchange:

ROLLING STONE: Doesn't your attendance give credence to John Lennon's comment that the Beatles were more popular than You?

JESUS: Not at all. Besides, We—My Father and I—felt certain the Antichrist, to bring misery and disillusion to the youth of the world, would soon rent the band asunder.

ROLLING STONE: Um, are You saying Yoko Ono is the Antichrist?

JESUS: "Well, *duh!*" sayeth the Lord.

MARK STEINES: It was right after Jesus' press conference that *ET*'s own Jann Carl caught up with the Man-slash-Son of God of the Hour for a one-on-one chat. Jann....

JANN CARL: Thanks, Mark. Though He'd had a grueling day of preaching, teaching, meditating, healing, and a little light carpentry, it was a tanned, rested, almost serene, Jesus Christ that I spoke with earlier today...
Is it all right to say You look fantastic, Lord?

JESUS: Of course, Jann. Thank you.

JANN CARL: I'm surprised, though. Your whole look has changed. For one thing, Your Hair is quite a bit shorter than in the pictures we're all so familiar with. And then there's Your Beard. Or should I say "lack of Beard?" Tell me, what possessed you—after what, two-plus millennia—to shave? Because honestly, if it wasn't for the stigmata, I'm not sure I'd even recognize you.

JESUS: My appearance is of no consequence. Perhaps—

JANN CARL: No consequence to *You* maybe, but I think I saw several hundred women out there today who disagree. I want to get serious for a minute, though. In the past, You've done a lot of healing. And today, probably the single person who could most use Your help in the whole world is the courageous Christopher Reeve. Any chance You might lay hands on him?

JESUS: I would like to see an end to all suffering.

JANN CARL: How about healing Sharon Osbourne? Or Mohammad Ali?

JESUS: The Champ's people called. We'll have to see. Right now, our schedules conflict. And then there's the little matter of his name…

JANN CARL: Now, we all understand that You're a man of love, a man of peace, a man of forgiveness. So tell our viewers, what exactly does Jesus Christ do for fun?

JESUS: Well, until recently, I enjoyed playing Yahtzee with Mahatma Gandhi.

BOB GOEN: We'll have more of our exclusive interview with the Messiah—including His startling explanation of what the hell He's doing here and how frightened we all should be—on tomorrow's *Entertainment Tonight*. Plus, go behind the scenes on the latest reality show, *American Religious Idol*. We hope you'll join us then.…

40 } Aesoptional

As a child, my favorite book was an oversized, illustrated edition of *Aesop's Fables*. Again and again, I would turn to these simple stories of wisdom and principle, absorbing the timeless truths set down by this ancient Greek author while simultaneously wondering how a tortoise could possibly speak intelligibly without benefit of lips.

As a young man, I discovered *Fables for Our Time* by James Thurber. In it, Thurber spins society, spouses, and bottomless highballs into updated, whimsical allegories that are not only wittily sophisticated but elegantly trenchant. As a budding writer myself, I could see the famed Algonquin Round Tabler's style and sensibilities were something I could never hope to duplicate. But I did consider the overall concept of fable updating to be totally rip-offable.

What follows is that rip-off. And while the tales you're about to read may lack the wisdom of Aesop as well as the urbanity of Thurber, I feel confident that in a country mad for *Maxim* magazine, syndicated courtroom TV shows, and deep-fried Twinkies, this won't be a huge problem.

The Spider and the Fly

"Have you ever thought about selling this place?" the fly asked the spider. "I mean, this web, in this neighborhood, I think it'd go pretty fast. You'd probably do darn well for yourself, too."

"Do you think so?" the spider asked.

"I know the market's very active right now. More buyers than sellers."

"Hmmm," the spider mused. Then, "You could be right, I suppose, but, I don't know, I'm not 100 percent sure I *want* to sell, to move right now."

"I hear you, Ms. Spider. I do. This is a big decision. A tough one. And I'm not trying to make it for you. But think about it: Can you afford *not* to sell? I mean, the kids are grown and gone. You've eaten your husband. You've got a lot more web here than you need…"

"I know, but this is my home. I'm comfortable here. I love my neighbors, my garden. The food supply is fabulous. Did I tell you that last year I was still eviscerating moths in *November*? Who still has moths in November?"

"I'm not arguing with you. You've got a great place here. But you and I both know, Ms. Spider, that, as time goes on, it's only going to get harder to keep up with. The maintenance. The repairs. And forgive my saying so, but your silk glands aren't getting any younger, am I right?"

"They *are* stiff in the mornings anymore. I swear, sometimes it feels more like I'm spinning hemp twine," the spider admitted.

"Exactly my point. But out at Gossamer Retirement Village that's a nonissue. Out there, you'd still have your own web residence but smaller, more suited to your lifestyle and the spinning's all done for you. Your evening meals are pre-eviscerated, too, and served to you in the communal feeding lair," the fly said. "Plus, think about this, you'd be living with a lot of arachnids your own age, with your same interests. That's part of the beauty of a senior community. Not to mention the security issue. Like the brochure I gave you says, 'Live with friends you haven't met yet. In a bird-free environment.'"

"I don't know..." the spider hedged.

"And think about this: If, God forbid, something should happen to you, say you lose a leg or two, or even four or five, to some human kid with a cruel streak, an Assisted Living Center is part of the Village. Ready to take care of you till you're back on however many appendages you have left."

"But I like my independence..."

"Sure you do. And no one's asking you to give it up. Just the opposite. You're free to come and go, mix or not mix, as much as you like," the fly pressed. "Come on. Let's go out to the Village and take a look around. Just a look."

"I'm an eyeless spider," the spider said.

"I'm sorry. Of course, you are. I knew that. Come take a *feel* around," the fly parried.

"Well, I guess it wouldn't hurt to just *feel,*" the spider conceded.

"Sure. I'll give you the tour, then we can go to my office and I'll outline the various plans and costs. Like I say, with what you'll get for this web, I'm sure I can make the financials work. Then I can help you fill out an application and get you on our list," the fly buzzed. "So why don't you undo me from this old webbing I'm stuck in here and I'll show you the way out to Gossamer...?"

MORAL: *The food chain is a lot more complicated than it used to be.*

Mr. Crow and Ms. Coyote

Mr. Crow was dining on a lifeless, luckless rattlesnake in the middle of the northbound lane of Route 43. As he stripped a stringy piece of flesh from an exposed rib, his old nemesis, Ms. Coyote, appeared on the narrow gravel berm.

"Let me guess," she smirked, "it tastes like chicken."

"Given my species' underdeveloped sense of taste," Mr. Crow replied, "I couldn't say."

MORAL: *Irony is lost on a crow.*

The Mouse and the Elephant

One day as Miles Mouse was walking home from his job at the research laboratory, he suffered shortness of breath and severe chest pains. *I thought the lab docs were injecting my brain with caffeine to grow cancerous tumors; how come this feels like I'm having a heart attack?* he thought, at which point he lost consciousness and keeled over.

Quite by coincidence, Quincy Elephant was out for his evening constitutional when he happened to see Miles succumb. Quincy, who had no formal medical training but who had attended a CPR class at the local Y, dashed over to help the stricken rodent. Unfortunately, when Quincy tried to expel air from Miles by pressing down on his chest with his front feet, he flattened the little omnivore to the thickness of a tortilla chip. Worse, operating on a full charge of adrenaline, Quincy didn't immediately notice his *faux pas.* So, continuing, he pinched off Miles's nose, put his trunk over Miles's mouth and blew an elephantine blast of air into Miles's lungs. Miles exploded.

Dr. Sheldon Hyena, the district coroner, testified in court that it if it weren't for the pachyderm's actions, Miles probably would have survived what was, the autopsy revealed, only an angina attack. Citing Section 346.9 of the Penal Code of the Jungle, the presiding magistrate ordered Dr. Hyena and his staff to eat Quincy.

MORAL: *Those classes at the Y are a waste of time.*

The Top Dog

In accordance with their Constitution, every four "dog years" (that is to say, every seven months in human time), dogs throughout the land hold an election of great importance. This election is for the office of Top Dog, Chief Executive of the canine population. Not so very many election cycles ago, as the early primaries were once again rolling around, a handsome and personable Golden Retriever named Rex decided he was just the fellow to fill this position, to be Top Dog.

"After all, I'm handsome, personable, and am comfortable barking in public," he said. "And besides, chasing stick just isn't as fulfilling as it used to be."

So Rex hit the campaign trail. Hit it hard. He began speaking to, smelling the buttholes of, and dry-humping registered voters in big cities and small towns everywhere. He addressed the crowds that gathered around overturned garbage cans and bitches in heat. He stumped at vet's offices and pounds. He worked like a dog and doggedly worked.

Unfortunately, Rex didn't have a defining message, one that would separate him from the rest of the pack. He, like nearly every other candidate, was against rolled up newspapers and baths. Just as predictably, he was a fervent believer in unlimited Snausages, the right to lick one's own genitals, and the death penalty for cats. With time running out and his campaign struggling, Rex came to the conclusion that to win he would have to find an issue he could own. That he could champion. At the same time, it would have to be one that wouldn't alienate any voting blocs or breeds.

His pollsters informed him that toy and small dogs rarely turned out at the polls. So, tailoring his appeal to larger breeds, he began speaking out on hip dysplasia, a disorder common among those fifty pounds and up. "I have seen the toll HD has taken on average working dogs," he told the crowds, "and I believe we as a species should do everything in our power to convince humans to eradicate it in our lifetime."

This issue, it turned out, was a home run for Rex. There was, of course, no pro-hip dysplasia candidate or organization, so there was no disapproval, no backlash, no negative consequences. And since no one could expect Rex—a dog, after all, just like them—to find a cure, he could be morally indignant, condemning the inaction of others without having to take any action himself. By the time his opponents saw that the issue was getting traction and declared their own positions, it was too late. So late, in fact, Rex began to publicly speculate on whether some of his "worthy adversaries" might be "soft on dysplasia." Come Election Day, Rex won in a landslide.

Seven months (or four dog years) later, with absolutely no change in domesticated animal violence rates, Snausage consumption levels or bathing intervals, with cats still flaunting their catness with impunity, and hip dysplasia still uncured, the whole Top Dog election process was repeated and Rex won a second term.

MORAL: *Dogs are obviously idiots but damn if they haven't streamlined the process.*

The Opossum Family

Every day, Mama Opossum got up early. Very early. Because Mama Opossum had so very many young and so very much to do.

First, Mama Opossum had to wake up all of her sixteen sleepy children and fix them breakfast. After breakfast, she had to clean up the kitchen while making sure everyone got dressed and ready for school on time. Then, she loaded all of the children in her pouch and set off.

Unfortunately for Mama Opossum, even though her young were all the same age, they were not all in the same grade and did not all get taken to the same school. Four of her youngsters were differently-abled and had to be dropped at a special needs school. Two others had scored unusually well on standardized tests and were enrolled in The Academy for Gifted Marsupials clear across the forest. Two children went to two different magnet schools, one emphasizing athletics (with especially strong Scurrying and Australian Possum Rules Football programs), the other teaching a curriculum in the creative and performing arts.

After Mama Opossum had made all five morning stops, she went off to her job as a waitress at the City Dump (which, in earnings and status, is, roughly, the opossum equivalent of being a product brand manager at a top packaged goods company). Then, at 3:00 every afternoon, she picked her sixteen kids up, making the five stops all over again.

Depending on the day of the week, other stops followed. Soccer practice, baseball practice, swimming, gymnastics, karate class, ballet class, skiing lessons, riding lessons, music lessons, physical therapy, doctor's appointments, the dentist, the fur stylist, play dates, birthday parties, the library, tutoring, recitals, etc. On weekends, things got a bit busier.

When Mama Opossum wasn't running the kids around, she was running errands and doing chores for the household (her helpmate had been gone two months, either, she'd concluded, accidentally flattened by a car or purposely flattened by a car), shopping, dropping off, picking up, cooking, cleaning, vacuuming, laundering, paying the bills, and everything else today's modern opossum family might request and/or require.

In the very rare moments Mama Opossum actually had to herself, she would unwind with a few fermented grapes that she kept in the fermented grape rack in the kitchen, and go out into the quiet night air and call to a female friend or one of her own thirteen siblings or her Mom, telling them how crazy busy she was and how she'd love to get together sometime soon but, given her schedule, she didn't know when that might be and that, more often than not these days, she felt like she was being pulled in a hundred different directions and that her life wasn't her own.

"But it's all stuff the kids want to do and things that have to get done," she informed them. "So what choice do I have?"

MORAL: *Jesus Christ, we are all so tired of hearing about your fucking schedule.*

The Clever Tuna

Late one morning, four fishermen were hauling in their nets. About halfway into the task, they brought an enormous catch of tuna on board. As the crew began extricating the fish from the net with hooked poles, one of the tuna, quite unexpectedly, spoke to them.

"Wait, fishermen," she said, "I am a wise and learned fish with knowledge of many things. If you will promise to return my companions and me to the sea, I shall answer one question, any question at all, from each of you to your complete satisfaction. If, though, I fail to fulfill my promise, I will guide you to the most multitudinous school of tuna in the sea, which shall earn you an inestimable fortune at the fish market."

The fishermen, reasoning any tuna that tossed around words like "multitudinous" and "inestimable" must be wise and learned, indeed, accepted the terms of her proposition.

"Tell me, Tuna, what is the meaning of life?" asked one. And she told him.

"Is Certs a breath mint or a candy mint?" asked another. And she told him.

"How can I lose weight without cutting down on the food I eat and yet not increasing my amount of exercise, either?" the third inquired. And she told him.

Finally, it was the fourth and last fisherman's turn. He turned to the tuna and, with furrowed brow, inquired:

"How does Leno keep beating Letterman in late night?"

MORAL: *Tuna steaks, on special, $6.99 a pound.*

41} A Brand New Denouement

Epilogue

I didn't see Marcus after that summer. Not because I held him responsible for my severed optic nerve but simply because I *had* a severed optic nerve, something which kept me from seeing anybody or anything. But we didn't talk, either. And for all I knew, Marcus could have moved. Or died. Or been keeping very, very quiet while in my immediate vicinity.

Strangely, despite what had happened, I found myself going alone to the bars and dives, the saloons and taverns, the inns and roadhouses, the bistros, the pubs, the cafés where we'd spent so much time getting "detox-qualified" together. Somehow, though, our old watering holes seemed less spirited. Less congenial. Less gratifying. Less like a frat house with a coin-op pool table and aging prostitutes. Then again, I asked myself, how could I be sure? I mean, how could I know, I wanted to know, if the changes I perceived were real or simply further evidence of a failing short-term remembering function of my head organ?

It was about two years after I began these excursions that, on a bitter cold Tuesday in March—the same month which, at one time, Marcus and I used to think was so much fun but which, for a while now, has been trying way too hard—I walked into Gus's for a quick one. No sooner had I pushed the door open than I heard, "You make me want to throw up, Gus. And I mean that in a good way."

That velvet voice. That sweetly regurgitative sentiment. Who else could it be but Chloe Pluribusunum, the come-hither bulimic Marcus had nearly married, divorced, and remarried? She'd all but disappeared after the failure of our armed coup attempt on the Symbionese Liberation Women's Auxiliary.

I slid onto the stool next to hers at the bar. She smelled of latex and isotopes. Like always.

"Gus, give Al here a Taliban Martini," Chloe said, before I could even get out, "Hello." Gus, strictly a shot and beer bartender, must've been stumped because I didn't hear him take a step or ice a glass.

"It's just like a regular martini," Chloe explained, "but instead of olives, you garnish it with the eyes of an infidel." His mission now clear, Gus sprang into action.

"What're you up to these days, Chloe?" I asked.

"Well, to pay the bills, I'm working at GarGownTua, the dress shop for plus-sized ladies down at the mall. But remember way back when you, me, and Marcus had that car pooling operation for smalltime bank robbers who couldn't afford to pay a full share to a wheelman? How I was always talking about someday being an actress? I'm finally getting my chance with a community theater group. I go to all their performances and act like I'm enjoying myself. Maybe we could go together some night?"

"Nah. Thanks anyway." I told her. "To me, theater's too much like watching TV with your wife holding the remote." She laughed. Was it sincere? Or had she become that good an actress?

I hadn't heard Gus set my drink down but I was pretty sure he had because I could feel it staring holes through me. "I'm glad to hear you're keeping out of trouble, though," I told her.

"Absolutely," she said. "Which is more than I can say for old Marcus," she added.

I asked what she meant by that.

"Heard he was never the same after that last business you guys pulled with the celebrity kidney stones. Picked up a serious Tylenol #5 habit—you know, the ones with codeine and the chewy caramel center. Then, a couple days ago he gets all loopy on 'em, runs a red light, and kills these Siamese twins who're in the middle of the crosswalk. Cops've got him locked up while they try to decide whether to charge him with one or two counts of vehicular homicide. Supposedly, he's so depressed they put him on suicide watch but with the jail being so understaffed and everybody's time so tight, they're just videotaping him then watching it on fast forward later."

Marcus? A drug addict? A killer? A criminal? Locked up? Suicidal? Hmm. Given everything that had gone before, I guess just about anybody could have predicted that.

42 } Smart with Pain

This section of the test is designed to test your reading comprehension. Completely read the paragraphs below. When finished, answer the questions that follow. Or, for those of you whose massive student brains have figured out we test makers are absolutely defenseless against clever bastards such as yourselves and that it'll be faster and easier to skip right to the questions and then scan the densely packed text for answers, well, you're not even reading this anymore because you're unfairly looking ahead, so why don't the rest of you also go on and get started . . . . **NOW.**

In 1987, Sam Benson was convicted on twelve counts of armed robbery and three counts of legged robbery (bank security cameras showed him brandishing a .38 revolver with his left foot). He was subsequently sentenced to over three hundred years in jail. His attorneys, Ross Phillips, a perfectly healthy but lethargic public defender who'd recently won the right in Federal Court to make his approaches to the bench in a golf cart, and Skeeter Marsh, Benson's brother-in-law who, based on his bar scores, was enjoined from questioning witnesses on any subject other than their lunch plans, appealed the decision on the grounds that Benson could not be reasonably expected to live three hundred years. But Messrs. Phillips and Marsh, rather than ask the court to overturn or shorten their client's sentence, instead demanded that every possible human effort be made to ensure their client survive his full three centuries of incarceration. Phillips argued in court that this was necessary to carry out the express wishes of the jury. (What the attorney did not reveal was that he was trying to provide for his son, Ross Phillips, Junior, a student at Holy Crap, I'm in Law School College of Law in Trenton, New Jersey, by building a long-term client base for whom the boy could file endless briefs and motions.) The court, their hands tied by the precedent of (Smoldering Josef) Frazier versus (Manny) Ali (commonly known as the Big Grudge in Front of the High Judge) granted the motion. As a result, Benson was remanded to the Maximum Security Wing of the Kokopelli Spa and Retreat for Healthful Living in Scottsdale, Arizona, to serve out the (by this time) remaining 297 years of his sentence.

Benson's years at Kokopelli were a total nightmare. He loathed the low fat/low sodium/high fiber diet that, while it included the familiar spoiled fruits and vegetables of his old prison, eschewed the spoiled meat he craved; he detested the yoga that promoted flexibility and serenity rather than weight-training's intimidating buffness; and he was baffled by a spa economy that was based not on the trading of cigarettes but the trading of seaweed wraps.

It was during his time at Kokopelli, however, that Benson, made an important personal breakthrough. During a sexual liaison with the facility's pool boy, Herman Calypso (who, it was common knowledge, was Benson's "spa wife"), the prisoner had a distinct-yet-vague flashback of physical and sexual abuse. Through work with the staff life-regression counselor, he was able to pinpoint a specific, heinous incident as well as the perpetrator—his stepfather, Phil DeLong. This carnal violation, Benson felt certain, was what had led him to a life of crime. Based on his horrific recollection, he filed a civil law-suit against DeLong, seeking the unprecedented sum of five thousand seaweed wraps in damages.

But, for several reasons, his lawsuit did not succeed. First, the alleged abuse took place at Benson's forty-second birthday party, at which time his stepfather was a frail eighty-nine and confined to a wheelchair. Second, dozens of witnesses said the "attack" was simply Mr. DeLong attempting to give his "boy" a "birthday spanking." Third, by his forty-second birthday Benson already had eight robberies under his belt. Finally, not only had DeLong been dead for six years when the lawsuit was filed, Sam Benson had been sole heir to his estate.

Today, Benson remains in Kokopelli, an embittered seventy-one-year-old man who, honest to God, doesn't look a day over fifty.

[Mark the correct answers to these questions on your answer sheet.]

1. Sam Benson's lawyers are:

    a. Scum.

    b. Bastards.

    c. Bloodsuckers.

    d. Good providers, just like Daddy.

2. The most predictable reference in the prison portion of the story is to:

    a. Anal sex.

    b. Bodybuilding.

    c. The cigarette economy.

    d. President George W. Bush's disregard of civil and human rights in the incarceration of terrorist "suspects" at Guantanamo Bay (implied).

3. Why is every imaginable business in the Southwestern United States named after Kokopelli?

    a. It's the law.

    b. It saves valuable thinking time for business owners.

    c. Who doesn't like Kokopelli?

    d. It beats commercializing and diminishing *Christian* beliefs.

4. Sam Benson's story would be a lot more interesting if:

    a. It was about Johnny Depp.

    b. It was an audiobook.

    c. He died at birth.

    d. IF!?...That's all your hot-shit grown-up world has to offer me? A big fat fucking "if"?

5. Blow this standardized test and you will:

    a. Mock the dorks who didn't.

    b. Commit hara-kiri (Japanese test version only).

    c. Go to football practice after school like always.

    d. Wonder if your answer to this question was the clincher.

43} Card-carrying Capitalist

Dear Mr. Woodwiff,

If you're like most people, you have dreams. Big dreams. Maybe you'd like to drive a car luxurious enough to compensate for your lack of a viable personality. Or enjoy an indulgent getaway to a far-flung land with an unconscionably low age of sexual consent. Perhaps you dream of going under-ground for a few years in order to stalk vile abortionists. Or could it be you've outgrown your taste for gaudy jewelry and are ready to make the leap to garish?

Well, whatever it is you're dreaming of—unless you're dreaming of boring old financial security—it can now be yours* when you carry one of the three prestigious new **MetaMetallic Visa Cards** from **ChaseCapital Bancorp.**

What's "MetaMetallic"? A class of card that transcends the traditional credit card "metals." Cards that outshine the tarnished luster of gold. That go beyond the tepid perks of platinum. That even make the entitlements of titanium seem humdrum.

To carry a ChaseCapital MetaMetallic Visa is to carry a credit card with the **unprecedented power**

to gratuitously impress. Each time you remove it from your wallet or purse, you'll instantly demonstrate to retail clerks, hotel and restaurant employees, travel agents, almost *any* minimum-wage worker or ambient stranger just how very **privileged** and **successful** you are. It's like buying respect with every purchase.

Our three distinctive MetaMetallic Visas, each with its own **exclusive benefits, staggering line of credit,** and **distinctively haughty cachet,** offer you the unique opportunity to select the card best suited to your **advantaged lifestyle.** Which card is right for you? Only *you* can decide.**

The Plutonium Visa—Experience the explosive purchasing power of the Plutonium Visa and you'll discover that the only thing it deters is a zero balance on your monthly statement. But this Visa isn't just everyplace you want to be, it's everyplace you've never been allowed before. Because the Plutonium Visa provides holders with the highest national security clearance offered by the United States Government. So you'll have access to everything from the FCC lab that's trying to figure out how 150 cable channels only generate four decent shows a week, to the Bethesda Naval Hospital room where Richard Nixon's five o'clock shadow remains alive after being grafted onto the face of a lingering, comatose JFK. Low monthly payments can be spread out over the half-life of the card or seventy-eight million years, whichever comes first. Benefits also include: Ground Zero-Billing, a waiver of your monthly bill should you become unemployed due to atomic warfare; unlimited admissions to Six Flags Over Toxic Barren Soil, the Utah theme park built atop a nuclear waste site; and a DVD of *Silkwood*.

The Scrimshaw Visa—The Scrimshaw Visa harkens back to a bygone era yet is loaded with contemporary benefits designed for today's "compassionate conservative." Carved from 100% whale ivory (purchased on the black market from Japanese poachers) and beautifully handcrafted by underemployed Inuits, this elegant credit card imbues the rich and powerful with even more riches and power. And perks? Plenty. With the Scrimshaw Visa, you'll be entitled to automatically upgrade any three (3) convicted felons residing in any of ten (10) high-security prisons from "life" to "lethal injection." Plus, your card serves as a concealed-carry handgun permit in all fifty states. And, for an introductory period of six months, we'll bill women's purchases at a "glass ceiling" rate of seventy-three cents on the dollar. You also have access to a $25,000,000 equity line of credit on each oil well you own or operate on land formerly designated as a "preserve," "forest," "sanctuary," or "park," plus an interest rate keyed to the "city gas mileage" of the average suv (currently a low, low 11.8 mpg, or 11.8 percent APR).

The Holy Grail Visa—Here's a card that's truly Divine. Blessed and/or consecrated by your choice of the Pope or Billy Graham, you'll always "Go (shopping) with God." The Holy Grail Visa also provides you with the protection of our CPAs or Clergified Public Accountants, a twenty-four-hour toll-free support team that quickly resolves merchant disputes in your favor by invoking the Irrefutable Law of God. Our MannaPoints Program awards you one MannaPoint for every dollar you spend and can be redeemed for dishwasher-safe chalices, monogrammed hair shirts, *The OT on CD* as read by Fran Drescher, and hundreds of other MannaPoints catalog items. Your HG Visa also features an exclusive Congregational Concierge Service that will make your arrangements for hard-to-get-into afterlife venues. As a card holder, you'll also be eligible to attend monthly services where you can join other faithful and devoted spenders in an endeavor to "pray down" interest rates.

So what are you waiting for? As a North American with a permanent mailing address and not residing south of the Mexican border, you're already

preselected, prepreferred, preevaluated, pre-thought-well-of, and **preapproved.** Simply complete the enclosed application and return it in the **prepaid** envelope. Soon, you'll be flashing and flaunting your MetaMetallic Visa the world over. Fulfilling your dreams of a better life. Or, worst case, believing you are.

Sincerely,

Bill Zoutyerass
Vice-President, Perpetual Marketing

*Other dreams expressly excluded from offer of fulfillment include: spiritual insight; love of family; living forever; a higher IQ; a reliable, affordable American car; and Jim Belushi going away any time soon.

**Final credit approval and assignment of MetaMetallic card type determined solely by ChaseCapital Bancorp.

44 } Bad Times Made Gooder

"How sound is the current U.S. economy?" the journalist asks the government official, the economist, the securities analyst, the corporate auditor and a host of other financial experts from A (accountants) to Z (zombie accountants). And from the interviewees comes, "It depends on which indicators you look at...," "If production and consumption remain strong into the next quarter...," Current trends appear favorable though not necessarily encouraging..."—all weak and waffle-y preambles that alert us we're getting a "response" as opposed to an "answer."

Not here. No, sir. From me, an accredited GAT (Guy Advancing a Theory), the same question is answered forthrightly. Unequivocally. Indisputably. "Due to the explosion in budget deficits and the wholesale outsourcing of U.S. jobs overseas, our economy's prospects are more tenuous than Grandma's bladder control."

With that issue settled, let us return to the experts and the journalist.

"Can anything be done to bolster recovery and stimulate the overall economy?" the reporter probes.

This time, there are no qualified replies. No, this time, we're earwitness to some highly confident answers. Firm answers. Predictable, hackneyed, partisan answers. "Clearly, another round of tax cuts...," drone those who lean right. "More spending on government-financed programs...," pronounce those who lean left. "Through the promotion of private investment...," declare the Wall Street touts. "By bombing Swiss competitors of U.S. businesses…," insists the CFO of American Cuckoo Clock, Inc.

To which I reply, "Hah!" "Bah!" "Pshaw!" and "Wha…?" respectively. My apolitical, impartial GAT conclusion is both obvious and reiterative: "Due to the explosion in budget deficits and the wholesale outsourcing of U.S. jobs overseas, our economy is as resistant to stimulation as the part of Grandma's plumbing I can't quite bring myself to mention by name."

But let me quickly add that such a dire prediction is really no cause for despair. Even the worst economic conditions can be handily, if not happily, endured with the right plan in place. As a survivor of several cyclical downturns, recessions, bear markets, deflations, slumps, slides, stagnations, stagflagtions, and one particularly tricky derecesslumflationruptcy, I offer these proven strategies and techniques as my gift to today's (and tomorrow's) economic victims:

1. **Do cut back. Don't cut out.** With wages relatively flat and expenses like health care continuing to skyrocket, money may be tight but denying yourself entirely is a prescription for failure. Scaling back is a much more effective approach. For instance, order your pie *sans à la mode*. Drop horseback riding for piggyback riding. Instead of filling and refilling your vehicle with expensive gasoline, start pushing it to your destination. Replace costly high-class hookers with budget-friendly crack whores.

2. **Safeguard your investments.** Today's market has as many plunges as it has peaks and is no place for the unsophisti-

cated, non-plugged in, part-time investor like you. This is the time to park your money in safer, proven investments. Like deposit bottles and Beanie Babies. Another hedge against uncertain times is precious metals; unfortunately, as their name implies, the cost of entry is prohibitive. Suggestion: Fill your portfolio with the so-called bourgeoisie metals: manganese, bismuth, and, molybdenum.

3. Sue somebody. Stop kvetching about this being the age of frivolous lawsuits and go cash in on one, dingus. Did your restaurant coffee burn your tongue? Sue. Is the water company supplying your house with a clear, odorless liquid that has the potential to drown you? Sue. Did your oldies station play "Bette Davis Eyes" and you can't get it out of your head? Sue. Most importantly, if you lose your case, don't give up hope. Go find a lawyer to sue your lawyer.

4. Remain bold. This is no time to stop playing the lottery or cut back on gambling. After all, if you don't win the rent, *who will?*

5. Swallow your pride…and your principles. If you find yourself out of work, be ready to take whatever comes along. Too often people think they're socially, educationally, and/or ethically "above" a certain kind of work. To that I say, where would this great country be if every *Cats* touring company, every Mary Kay representative, every Mrs. Donald Trump felt the same way?

6. Think "outside the job box." If unemployment persists, don't get discouraged. Working is just one of dozens of ways to earn a living. There's also begging. Come on, if that scraggly, mean-looking drunk who's been sitting outside your (former) office building for the past two years can do it, how hard can it be? Or how about stealing? Stealing is a vocation that's highly entrepreneurial, offers flexible hours, and has a rich, colorful history dating all the way back to some Greek who's name escapes me stealing some item I can't recall from some god that's slipped my mind. For those lacking the thief's temperament, there's drug dealing, kidnapping, usury, blackmail, fraud... Well, the number of profitable choices is almost criminal. And don't forget this little fact: when unemployment is up, payrolls are down; when payrolls are down, municipal tax revenues are down; and if tax revenues are down, *police ranks are also down*. Meaning whichever felonious field you choose, your chances of arrest actually *decrease* as the economy worsens. Before long, you'll kick yourself for not wandering from the straight and narrow years ago.

7. Define "essential services." In the event current conditions should worsen, you might consider disconnecting some utilities. For instance, go ahead and drop your phone service, after all, nobody's going to call a broke, jobless loser like you. By the same token, since you no longer need to shower for work, water is expendable. Just remember, unemployment is *really* boring, *ergo,* your cable TV service should be the last to go.

One final word of advice: Keep the faith. Unless you think you can get a few bucks for it on eBay.

45 } Sometimes a So-So Nation

Business Plan, Phase 1—Inception. Steal or duplicate an idea for a product or service. Allow idea to gestate as you delude self into thinking that the very traits that make you a poor employee will make you a good entrepreneur. Enthusiastically share the idea with several close friends who declare it a dead-on, can't-miss winner, but in reality simply don't have the heart to tell you they think it's a dead-end, stone cold loser. Earnestly explain it to group of professional colleagues who are so nonplussed you actually look up nonplussed in the dictionary to find out if it means what you think you remember it means. Outline idea to brother-in-law who clucks and frowns discouragingly while simultaneously plotting to steal or duplicate idea for self. Move mindlessly forward.

Business Plan, Phase 2—Financing. Implore loving family to float you a low- or no-interest loan. Up ante by offering loving family equity stake in return for low- or no-interest loan. Declare whole shortsighted, tightfisted family "dead" to you. Write business and/or marketing plan. Submit plan to Bank A as part of business loan application. Learn application has been turned down; drown sorrows in fifth of cheap scotch. Creatively rewrite business and/or marketing plan. Submit plan to Bank B as part of business loan application. Learn application has been turned down; drown sorrows in fifth of cheap scotch. Spin web of carefully crafted lies, treachery and deceit into a business and/or marketing plan. Submit plan to Bank C as part of business loan application. Learn application has been approved; celebrate success with fifth of expensive scotch charged against your new line of credit.

Business Plan, Phase 3—Incorporation. Search for suitable commercial property to buy or lease. Contribute to suburban sprawl by locating new business on site of former forest/former farmland. Contribute to traffic congestion nightmare as well as sharp rise in air and noise pollution by attracting vehicled employees to area with woefully inadequate road system. Contribute absolutely nothing to local revenues and, by extension, local residents' quality of life, by extorting lucrative tax abatement from short-sighted, growth-at-any-cost suburban planning commission in exchange for locating business in their overdeveloped, over-congested, dirty, noisy neck of woods. Interview indifferent prospective workforce. Treat prospective workforce with indifference. Research progressive management and leadership techniques. Discard pointy-headed theories as so much claptrap. Embrace tried-and-true tradition of labor vs. management antagonism. Ratchet up "antagonism" to "antipathy." Institute policy of paying industry minimum wages; declare workplace nonunion. Grant self substantial pay raise for keeping payroll down and greedy, corrupt unions out. Buy and wear Kevlar vest.

Business Plan, Phase 4—Supply. Commit to producing highest possible quality at lowest possible price, where "highest" is defined as "not all that high" and "lowest" is defined as "not really very low." Set production goals. Start production. Stop production. Rework production. Restart production. Repeat "Start, Stop, Rework, Restart" process. Repeat "Start, Stop, Rework, Restart, Repeat" process. Initiate personal gastrointestinal analysis and comparison of relative effectiveness of Mylanta versus Maalox. Reassess initial production goals as overly ambitious. Push back first shipment date. Discover cost per unit much higher than anticipated: downgrade materials; actively ignore costly EPA and/or OSHA and/or FDA and/or FTC and/or comparable state agencies' guidelines; investigate bringing on undocumented workers/relocating to Southeast Asia. Push back first shipment date even further. Appeal to bank for additional money (ski mask optional). Use newly acquired capital to sustain production. Make first shipment. Continue production. Await new orders. Continue to await new orders. Note 5,000 percent increase in personal daily use of phrase, "I am *so* fucked." Create inventory of unsold product. Announce lay-offs. Trade up to Kevlar body suit with matching Kevlar hat.

Business Plan, Phase 5—Creating Demand. Meet with ad agencies. Shower vigorously. Hire ad agency; realize you are now part of the problem. Order agency to turn your cocktail napkin doodle into logo. Slap logo on everything except your children. Review and reject several proposed ad campaigns because they're "too risky, too edgy." Review and reject several proposed ad campaigns because they're "too blah, have no edge." Review and reject several proposed ad campaigns because they're "neither fish nor fowl, unclassifiable." Feel certain that idiots at ad agency think you're an idiot. Decide to star in own ads; fail to realize you are now part of whole other problem. Hire firm specializing in interactive communication and design to create and maintain yet one more humdrum, ineffectual, pointless corporate Web site in an infinite sea of same. Pledge to faithfully update Web site quaterly, unless business is too busy to fit it in or too slow to warrant it. Reconsider and rescind child logoization exemption.

Business Plan, Phase 6—Demand. Make a few sales. Make a few dollars. Show up on radar of large, powerful, deep-pocketed corporation. Stand helplessly by as large, powerful, deep-pocketed corporation launches product or service similar to yours but with slightly advanced design and/or more features and/or more benefits and/or more advantages for less money. Increase daily "I am so fucked" usage by additional 5,000 percent. Disbelieve. Tremble. Panic. Lower prices in last ditch attempt to protect and maintain market share. Enrage large, powerful, deep-pocketed corporation, triggering price cut impossible for small, weak, shallow-pocketed corporation to match. Lose market share. Yield market share. Surrender market share. Hemorrhage market share. Become dog-shit on sole of large, powerful, deep-pocketed corporation's shoe. Invite few remaining employees to house for combination job termination/skeet shooting party. Remove Kevlar suit.

46} Prospectus Interruptus

Past performance is no guarantee of future results. Legal disclosure should not be confused with actual disclosure. Publication of our phone number is not an invitation to call. This Prospectus's use of the English language is not intended to suggest to English-speaking Shareholders that the document is, in whole or in part, in any way comprehensible. Friendly, optimistic marketing materials do not typify the mood of individuals employed by our marketing department. Unindicted Fund management is not necessarily an indicator of ethical business practices. In the event of market downturn, failure of the Shareholder to experience orgasm should in no way be interpreted by the Shareholder as his or her *not* being totally screwed.

Expense examples are not representative of actual expenses. Maintenance fees are assessed through consultation of a Ouija board while biting down on a AA battery. Statistics contained herewith are intended for use in the formulation of a personal investment strategy but are just as effectively used when cut into confetti-sized pieces, placed in a hat, drawn and played as Powerball numbers. Figures in (parentheses) signify losses; figures in *italics* are numeric mimes performing "leaning against a wall;" figures in **bold** must submit to periodic random urine tests to screen for illegal steroids.

* * *

All fund holdings are subject to change. The spelling of the word "change" is subject to tchaing. Vowels included in the portfolio's holdings are purchased through commercial brokers and carry a 5 percent "Vanna Commission." *Full Yield* and *Total Distribution* are pet names of Fund-employed prostitutes. The Fund neither buys nor sells any wine before its time. Small-cap companies are defined as any publicly traded firm whose CEO has a hat size of less than 6 3/8 Russian investments are calculated in a ten-to-one ratio with dry vermouth. Risk-averse investors are urged to let go of Mommy's apron strings and quit making us all sick. Depending on context, the terms "bull market" and "bear market" may refer to the actual purchase of dressed bovine and ursine meat products for the sole purpose of grilling at the Fund's annual picnic.

Redemption of shares may result in a capital gain or loss. Redemption of your soul may result in loudly testifying for Jesus on public transportation. Failure to pay applicable federal, state, and local taxes on investment income may explain why you answer to the name "Leona." Current Fund share price information can be obtained by Shareholders with a touch-tone phone and a working mojo; transactions via the Internet will require your account number, a password, and far more time than you'd think. Minimum investments of $2,500 are payable by check or bank draft and should be made out to "The Guy With All The Beautiful $2,500 Suits." Fund investments are not backed or insured by the U.S. government, though the Treasury Department has agreed to compensate total losses with a free two-item medium Domino's pizza and a two-liter Pepsi. SEC regulations strictly prohibit mutual fund managers from requiring new investors

47 } Salvador Dolly Shot

dolly shot: Also called "travelling," "trucking," or "tracking shot." A moving shot of a moving or stationary subject accomplished by mounting the camera on a dolly or camera truck. To dolly-in (or track-in) is to move the camera toward the subject.

At the end of the driveway lies a long-ago fallen, decaying sycamore, home to a billion gnawing termites, none of them thinking it might be time to start taking a fiber supplement. A split rail fence dating back to the Civil War encircles the entire property and, as a valuable relic of the past, is itself protected from harm by a nasty, gleaming girdle of razor wire. Just inside this double perimeter, safeguarding the family vegetable garden, is an electrified chain link fence that not only carries enough voltage to fry small varmints, it's fully coated with Teflon II, so that cooked-on meat and singed fur clean-up quick and easy, without scratchy pads or harsh cleansers.

Across the adjacent countryside, weeds are growing like children.

A ravenous, taut-skinned cur approaches a ramshackle outbuilding, tips a proximate garbage can, ferrets a brittle wishbone from a chicken carcass, chomps it down, begins to choke, and, in fulfillment of his instinctive wish to dislodge the obstruction before it kills him, miraculously coughs it up, though the violence of his hacking ruptures a major artery and *that* kills him. The ancient hulk of a Cherokee is perched upon cinder blocks, silently cursing the white man for stealing this parcel of land from his tribal ancestors and leaving only cinder blocks for him to sit on.

An unexpected residence rises from the rolling landscape, an architectural jewel often credited to Eero Saarinen but in actuality the work of someone with a more plausible name. The home's beauty radiates a quiet solemnity, not unlike a urologist's office or a Jaguar dealer's showroom. A doormat lies at its threshold; the lie is "Welcome."

To enter the house is to be assailed by an overwhelming odor of mothballs, though their noxious bouquet is underscored by a heady musk of moth vaginas. The entry hall is ornate in its decoration, containing, among other things, an elephant foot umbrella stand, an impala antler coat rack, a secretary with extensive tortoise shell inlay, a zebra skin rug, a rhinoceros-hide steamer trunk, a floor lamp with a delicate scrimshaw base topped with a sharkshaw shade, and the original framed and signed Terms of Surrender agreed to by The Animal Kingdom.

Passing into a wide hallway, the eye is immediately drawn to the rich, sculpted, deep-pile wall-to-wall-to-wall-to-wall carpeting that graces both floor and ceiling. The walls themselves are painted a color that does not occur in nature or industry or art or science or science fiction or Oz or Hunter Thompson's medicine cabinet or God's dreams (affidavit on file); the trim is painted a full shade lighter than clear.

The living room is so relentlessly sunless, so unmercifully dark that one could not read Braille there without a flashlight. Along the far wall, built-in bookshelves hold trite bric-a-brac; various surfaces are cluttered with garish knickknacks;

on the west wall hangs an antique broadsheet for the comedy ice-skating team of Frick and Frack. (Unseen, deep in the far removes of the couch cushions, there lies a bonanza of spilled, stray Tic Tacs.) Overall, the impression is of a room decorated by either a hick or a hack.

Quickly up a flight of stairs, down another hall, past two bedrooms, a sitting room and a standing room only. Three full baths are available on this level, though their convenient accessibility is moot since all are built in only two of the available three spatial dimensions. Similarly, the house's many walk-in closets stand empty and useless by virtue of their being installed with no walk-*outs*.

To sleep in this home's master suite is to be returned to the comfort of the womb but with far lower humidity. This is where serenity resides, though it's not altogether clear if serenity's paying its own rent. The decor, the furnishings, the accoutrements couldn't be more united in character and purpose if they were folk singers at a labor rally. It seems likely that any dream occurring in this room would be filled with symbolism indicating the dreamer's unworthiness to sleep in this room.

Past the bed, a sliding door opens onto a deck so impeccably situated it seems to declare, "If I weren't here, instead of soaking in the view, you'd be plummeting to serious injury or death from outside a second story bedroom right now," which, impeccability be damned, still comes off as pretty cocky for a lousy deck. Down below, in the backyard, there's a *trompe l'oeil* in-ground swimming pool (which was impossible to pass up since it was no more expensive than the *trompe l'oeil* above-ground model) surrounded by a quartet of loungers painting their bodies with self-tanning lotion.

Beneath a clear blue sky, the sound of Tibetan chants floats on the air; so much so, it may be necessary to call Tibet and ask them to hold it down before you call the cops.

Cut. Print.

No. Wait. Make it cursive.

Bob Woodiwiss began his career as a writer/satirist at age seventeen. His first effort, a self-published parody of his high school's newspaper, earned him an eight-day suspension. Completely sapped and consistently stoned, Bob (subconsciously) decided to take a decade-long breather from the pressurized, punitive world of publishing.

In the ensuing years, Bob worked a variety of jobs, including bartender, cabinetmaker, truck driver, and unscrupulous high-pressure salesman of hope chest items for prospective brides. For two incredibly sooty and emphysemic years, he co-owned a chimneysweep company.

In 1983, frustrated with his series of mindless blue- and gray-collar jobs, Bob decided to enroll in college and earn a degree that could secure him a series of mindless white-collar jobs. He graduated with just such a degree in 1986.

Since that time, he has worked as an advertising copywriter and creative director; in 1992, he started his own firm, Bob, The Agency, which he still owns and operates. Over the course of his career, Bob's ads have garnered countless local, regional, and national awards, awards he'll try to remember as he burns in Hell for his soulless, shameless, unrepentant intrusion on and hornswoggling of the public.

In addition to his business, from 1994 until 2002 he wrote a satirical column titled *Pseudoquasiesque*, for *Cincinnati CityBeat*, an alternative weekly newspaper. His articles have been published in numerous other alternative papers nationwide, as well as *Stun* magazine and, somehow, swear to God, *Il Manifesto*, an Italian Communist newsweekly. In the spring of 2004, after a nearly two-year absence, he resumed his column for *CityBeat* under the title *Estrangement in a Strange Land*. Neither writer nor publisher is quite sure why.

Bob reluctantly lives and lives reluctantly in Cincinnati, Ohio.